Dear Jackie / Louise

With thanks and gratitude for your kindness in allowing us to stay in your Capesby cottage.

With love

Robert

Elements In Being

Illuminate your experience

Written by Robert Merrett
Illustrations by Sophie Merrett

Copyright ©2020
Robert Alexander Merrett

Illustrations copyright ©2020
Sophie Rebecca Merrett

First published 2020

All rights reserved
Without limiting the rights under copyright
Reserved above, no part of this publication may be reproduced, stored in or introduced into a retrieval system, or transmitted, in any form or by any means (electronic, mechanical, photocopying, recording or otherwise). Without the prior written permission of both the copyright owner and the publisher of the book.

www.elementsinbeing.com

First edition

Disclaimer.
Although the author and publisher have made every effort to ensure that the information in this book was correct at press time, the author and publisher do not assume and hereby disclaim any liability to any party for any loss, damage, or disruption caused by errors or omissions, whether such errors or omissions result from negligence, accident, or any other cause.

In memory of Frank

Even the briefest encounter can inspire action that changes a destiny.

For my family

No matter what you need right now,
all you require is waiting within.

Contents

Chapter One – Understanding Ourselves
What we are

Chapter Two - The Hub Elements
Element One : Reflection
Element Two : Attention

Chapter Three – The Space In-between
Element Three : Dreaming

Chapter Four - The Wheel Rim
Element Four : Connection

Chapter Five – The Spoke Elements
Element Five : Attraction
Element Six : Meaning
Element Seven: Intention
Element Eight : Gratitude
Element Nine : Loving Kindness
Element Ten : Forgiveness
Element Eleven : Courage
Element Twelve : Belief

Chapter Six - Implementation
Element Affirmations
Self-actualisation Affirmations
I Am Affirmation

Chapter Seven – Reflection
Reflections on Being

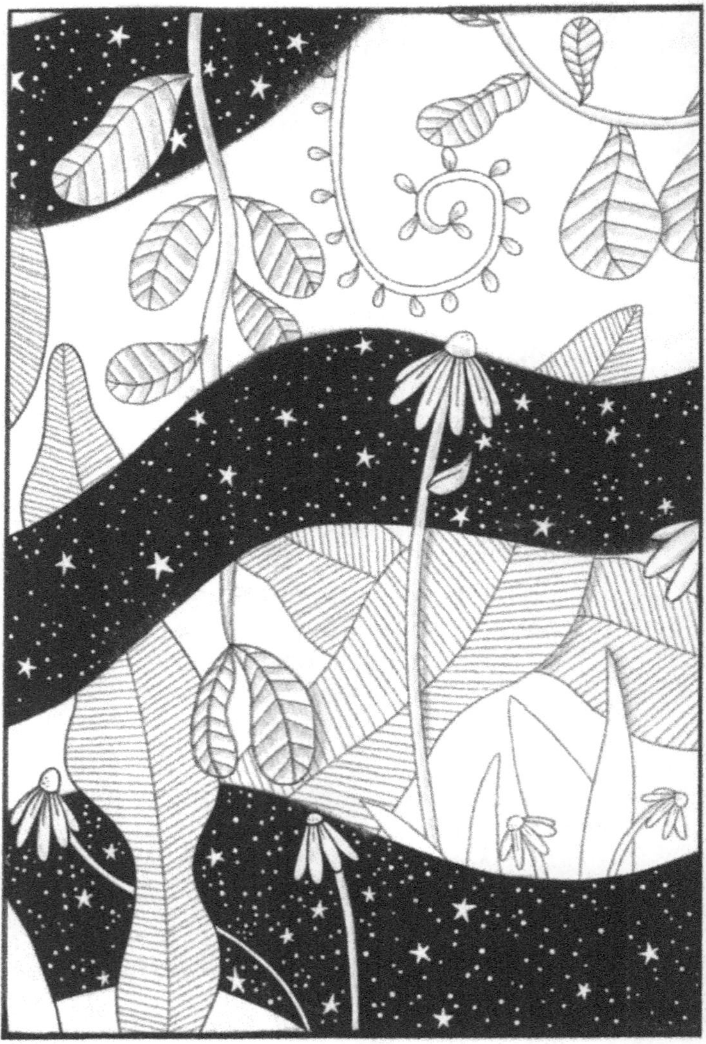

Introduction

All life is a circle and around it we go, though what it surrounds we do not know.

More than ever, a question we seem to ask ourselves in this modern life is: How do I find happiness?

Are you pursuing happiness but rarely find it or hold on to it for an appreciable amount of time?

The idea that you can search for happiness, as if looking for some lost item stored in a dusty loft is quite ridiculous, is it not?

Happiness at any rate cannot be pursued, it must ensue. It can only materialise from within your present moment. Finding it therefore must take place by immersing the senses exclusively, astonishingly, openly and gratefully into everything that comprises the moments of your life, as they occur.

If asking the question "How do I find happiness?" is somewhat ridiculous, you may be forgiven for thinking that you have been chasing an illusion. If this is the case then a more valuable, deeper and relevant question for our 21st century lives might be: How do I become content? You see, our pursuit of happiness is more often than not a misguided, half-cocked or haphazard orientation to what we sense we should be doing, should look like, or should be surrounded by, that typically leads to mere moments of brief joy, rather than what is so elusive to us; contentment.

Around two-thousand five hundred years ago Lao Tzu wrote of the importance of contentment above all else, translated here by Thomas Cleary:

"No crime is greater than discontent, no fault is greater than possessiveness. So, the satisfaction of contentment is always enough."
Verse 46, Tao Te Ching.

The very pursuit of happiness is something we must actually let go of if we are to become truly content. But it doesn't mean that we need to let go of experiencing joy. Ironically, the more we work to release our blind pursuit of happiness, the more likely we are to experience joy. Why? It's just another of life's paradoxes that, when you let go of your resistance to what you haven't got, what you were pursuing all along can materialise.

What you have been pursuing all along requires using what is already available within you; your Elements In Being. Discovering how to reach and use these inherent Elements is the intention of the book.

There are many snippets of past wisdom that I have drawn on that punctuate this book, though I trust that you will find it to be more than a book that recycles old adages and truths. It is a series of deliberate steps in your own self-searching discovery that provides guidance to contentment.

A continuous process of challenging your thinking and beliefs, of understanding the fundamental Elements within to create ever greater degrees of emotional resilience and emotional intelligence, as well as practical tasks to undertake that will create change towards becoming a more contented person.

I truly hope that as you read and then go through this self-searching process, that you will attain what has motivated you to pick up the book and read this far. To understand further, to work out completely what the book can bring to you, well I guess you will just have to continue.

At this stage you may be wondering whether you should spend your valuable time reading what seems to be yet another self-improvement / self-help book. If that's so, I understand how you feel, there are a lot of them around. It is a complex, infinitely variable subject with a seemingly unending goal, and on top of that you will be investing a reasonable amount of your precious time.

One of the greatest benefits in working through this book is that it increases your ability to manage your fears, stress and anxiety, in healthy adaptive ways. Fear is without doubt our necessary protector, but is also the steel chain which holds us back from many of life's greatest pleasures and advancements.

So, before you close the book and put it back on

the shelf, I'd like you to consider some of these biggest underlying difficulties that interfere with your life by asking yourself this:

If I only had one year to live, what would I do with my 365 days of time?
Who would I see?
What would I tell them?
What would I leave behind as my mark?
What kind of person would I like to be remembered as?

If you have managed to answer these questions:
What do you fear that is stopping you?
Change? Uncertainty? Rejection? Loss?
What is your reason for inaction?
What is the worst that could happen if you act?
365 days..... close your eyes and imagine that's all you have.

I understand that there may be financial or circumstantial barriers in being able to act, but these aside, don't skip too quickly over the questions. Give them the time and quality of thought that you and the questions deserve. Go into any fears you may have, don't just skim the surface.

Is there a person with whom you need to make amends but are afraid of what might happen? Go deeper and check just what is it that would be so bad. Perhaps you are afraid of showing your vulnerable self that might appear to show weakness or inferiority? Maybe you are unwilling to feel the hurt that could come from a possible rejection?

Whatever our fears, they rarely get examined in any degree of detail. So, go into your dark and examine what lies lurking there, rather than being in fear of it and unconsciously keeping the light on. Getting to the root of the fear is important if we are to overcome it.

Now consider if any of the following apply to you:

Do you feel there must be more to life than this?
Do you ever feel frustrated and at odds with your life and some of the people in it?
Do you feel a lack of passion, meaning or pleasure in your work, or do you do it because you have to?
Do you have a dream that never seems to get any nearer?
Are you in a relationship that is toxic and from which you cannot break free?
Do you sometimes feel as if fate is against you, that things always seem to go wrong?
Are you ever restless, stressed, anxious, in fear, feeling hopeless or worthless?
Are there times when it is impossible to shut down your worries, rumination or overthinking?
Do you believe you can become a better version of you?

If you answer "yes" to any of the above, then finding your own understanding of and working with the Elements in your Being will help enable you to address these problems.

Life issues such as those above and countless more are common to all of us, sometimes persistently, sometimes just for periods in our life. Often, we hide them from both ourselves and others. Rarely do we take a comprehensive, structured and detailed approach to the central aspects of ourselves that either empower or dis-empower us in addressing these matters. Indeed, when we are troubled by them, this is the very point in our life when attempting to understand ourselves is blocked by our embattled mental health. Tragically, for those who at the depths of their Being are suffering from histories of traumatic experience or a lack of loving, nurturing parental figures, the barriers to addressing these aspects of ourselves are significantly greater.

It is quite paradoxical that most of us are wise for others but not for ourselves. In a world of instant advice and unlimited information, we are bombarded with sound bites, inspirational quotes and memes that we love to share and ring bells of truth for us, but seldom do they penetrate to assist us much beyond the surface, or do we truly practice what they teach us. Despite that, this book is punctuated with them as a way of adding to the depth of the exploration within, or to provide summary to the descriptions of the Elements in Being. Like these quotes, stories also abound of others who have triumphed through adversity, become advanced practitioners of presence and contentment or who have found their calling. But these stories, these truths and sagely advice alone are like oil on water when it equates to getting to the deepest depths of the ocean of our self. To benefit from the advice they offer requires a self-searching effort, self-practice and persistent reflection.

In introduction, as well as laying out a reasonably succinct explanation of what the book is about, it is worth providing the background to how and why it has come to be written.

A few years ago, a humble, gracious and generous man, who was a highly distinguished professional under my therapeutic guidance, encouraged and even pleaded with me, on a number of occasions, to write a book of assistance for others such as himself, declaring that to not make available to a wider audience than himself the benefits of our work would be a travesty. I'm quite sure that this is far from a one-off example of such a request within the field of therapeutic relationships. Even so, I was of course flattered by his faith in me to put into my own words the kind of beneficial guidance he felt he was receiving. I may have easily dismissed this apparent flattery out of hand as is the duty of the therapist. Self-congratulation is not helpful for the therapist and it certainly doesn't benefit their clients, not least because it is the client who is making the changes, taking painful and difficult steps, and therefore the client who must own their beneficial work and thus increase their own self-love, self-determination and empowerment.

Despite this, deep down I knew this was not just a

request to flatter, but a combination of his own experiences of teaching and encouraging others, and the learnings that had been developed through our work together. It was also an example of this gentleman's nature; that of selflessly giving to others, often to the expense of giving to himself. So, to my client I simply pointed out that it would be impossible to create a work of his suggestion that would benefit the reader in anything more than a general way. I felt that to try and replicate the individual responses, attention, listening, nuances and detail of the therapeutic encounter would be impossible and make any book worthless. In such a format, this is absolutely true, but nevertheless I proceeded to put this seed, his idea, to the back of my mind and focus on writing in a more general way.

The benefit of planting seeds is that, with the right conditions, they find a way of growing don't they. Herein lies an important lesson. Ideas, or we might just say thoughts, if they are frequented enough, have the habit of growing. Whether these thoughts are good or bad, right or wrong, contented or sad, fearful or confident, they will perpetuate. If the conditions are also right, they flourish. But we will go through this in more detail further on in the book as it is integral to many of the Elements in Being.

As I reflected over the following years, what I realised was that my client's idea and my interpretation of it were quite different. What became apparent was that there are eternal truths

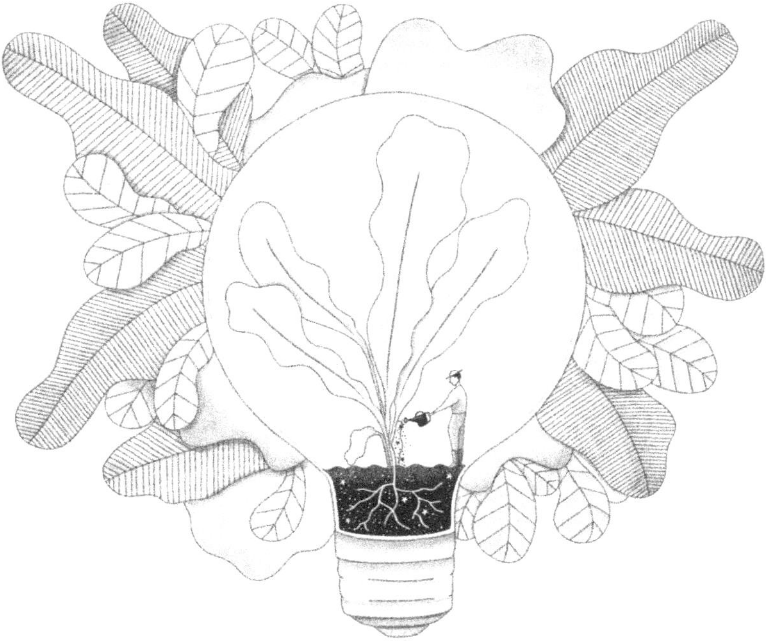

and processes, or Elements, relevant to all people in varying degrees, and that these, if conveyed in the right way and then understood and practised, can form a worthwhile resource for those who are struggling in their lives with matters of the heart and mind, for those who more generally want to develop their emotional intelligence, or for those who want to feel more content in their own skin and in their life.

What has transpired is designed to challenge. It is a form of human user manual in which a number of key Elements In Being are identified, honed, and then incorporated more beneficially into ones life. When they are practiced, important eternal truths can be learned, developed and understood through these key Elements in our Being which each one of us possesses. Learning about each Element, how to use them as a force for wellbeing, improving your awareness of them, and how they interconnect to work for or against you is an active part of the book.

Through the years I have spent counselling and coaching people experiencing life's problems, fears, anxieties, their addictions, losses and traumas, there has been a steady growth in my own experience of self-practice. This book has been a process of the formulation and solidification of my own understandings, the conceptualisation of the interplay of the Elements in my Being and the underlying force they have to power my thoughts, feelings and behaviours, and thus define both my destiny and level of contentment. The principles of acceptance, self-determination, cognitive behaviour therapy and mindfulness, of my own sense of spirituality and intuition and a large dollop of wise words from past mentors and teachers are all part of the mix.

Let's just say that we all need nourishment and exercise to be physically healthy and maintain our bodies, we have choices to make in the quality of what we feed ourselves and how we move our bodies, and in the same way, we also have choices in how we feed and exercise our emotional, non physical self and maintain a mentally healthy system.

It is my firm belief that investing in our mental health is at the leading edge of creating a healthy physical body and more importantly as the driving force towards a healthy physical world. Whether dealing with politics, climate change, environmental destruction, homelessness or the plethora of world issues we face, seeking solutions outside of ourselves will always fall short of success. The answers to our problems come from within by changing our addiction to cultures of Ego which serve as illusions of happiness, but constantly thwart our individual and global peace and contentment. It's ultimately up to us, but first we must decide to be ready and then:

"When the student is ready, the teachers will appear" Buddhist proverb.

Are you ready?

So far you will have gathered that Elements In Being is a book that aims to offer a form of beneficial guidance in developing and maintaining your own mental and emotional wellbeing. Never has this area been more topical, nor help more needed. The almost daily dosage of mental health campaigns, R U OK day, Mental health days and suicide awareness campaigns are not happening because mental health is improving in society, they are in response to the modern epidemic of depression, anxiety and ever increasing suicide rates which are bred from the way in which we now live ever more complex, disconnected, ego driven and uncertain lives.

As I have been writing, there has also become a deepening spiritual aspect to the book for me, something I suspected may happen and that cannot be sufficiently explained with words and which to me is undoubtedly inseparable from the purpose of it. It doesn't matter whether you consider these spiritual aspects to be a part of this process. If they are necessary for you then they will become 'visible' to you. The very nature of spirituality exists, if you believe it, in its own dimensional perspective, without a suitable language to describe it. Therefore, spirituality cannot be explained adequately enough to fit with our incredibly limited human perspective via English, or indeed any other language we could understand. As you look down the chapter headings though it is undeniable that each Element is incorporeal or without material form and therefore metaphysical.

Another of the precursors to the book being written is the overwhelming sense of change, loss, disconnection and self comparison that exists in our lives. I have felt, on a near daily basis, a requirement to pull together, for myself primarily, but also for any reader, an understanding of the Elements In Being which we have at our disposal, at any time, along with suggestions of how they may be effectively developed and used to deal with the challenges of modern life.

The book is also a guide to the deliberate and "cleansed" use of these Elements in our Being, which exist within every single one us, for the purpose of allowing us to be all that we potentially can be.

One of the greatest personal benefits of counselling and psychotherapy is not just experiencing the many differences in people, but experiencing the consistencies of people. Having the privilege of counselling all ages, shapes and sizes of human beings and 'hearing' their griefs, fears, traumas and depressions, often in their darkest hours, I know that in general, the essence of our human selves is universal.

As hard as it may seem in our world of personalities and celebrities, of winners and losers, you can be assured that the essence within all of us, underlying the story of ourselves is from the same elemental source. This is a great leveller, so no matter whether you are a President or Pauper, a Concierge or a Celebrity, this guide to each

Element will, when understood, followed and practiced, assist in maximising your full potential as a human being, no matter what your circumstances.

None of the Elements I describe and suggest in this context are new. How could they be if they are so intrinsic. They have been previously and extensively explored. They are drawn sometimes from the oldest of ideas, from wise sages, shamans and philosophers, poets and writers, scientists and those of religion. The task here is to work through and develop this advice in a useful way, from raw data, to information, to understanding, then insight, and finally to wisdom.

Realise that right now, at this very moment, you have the most extraordinary opportunity for inner peace. Everything is already within you, in place and waiting for your attention to shift.
There was never a time when that opportunity was not there. While you are still living, there will never be a time when the opportunity is gone.

This is not just about reading; it also requires working with the book as a process. As you work your way through, it develops and grows, interchanging from information to concepts to understandings and to practice. To help with this, I have split the book into chapters, some of which are symbolised by the various parts of a wheel. The wheel and its components illustrate the working functions and the position of each Element within the greater picture.

Chapter one is our starting point for self-examination, what we comprise in simple terms and what is important to observe in ourselves.

Chapter two describes the two Elements of Reflection and Attention that are at the hub of the wheel, central to the access of our wellbeing, the maintenance and the advancement of it.

Chapter three is our hidden space of potentiality, our creative Element of Dreaming, sitting in-between, always there waiting to form the blueprints of our future creations.

Chapter four singles out the Element of Connection, which is symbolised as the rim of the wheel, both the infinite never-ending circle and the interface with all other Elements.

Chapter five describes the other Elements in our being that expand and connect like spokes from our central hub of wellbeing.

Chapter six is an action plan for the Elements in your being. A clear schedule of affirmations to propel your Elements to the next level and develop deeper understanding, meaning and contentment in your life.

Chapter seven seeks to reflect on Being itself and embed into your life the new learnings and practices that will exist from a new consciousness.

I hope like me you are eager to explore the real

workings of the book, but before the introduction is over, I'd like to offer a few final thoughts as you begin your journey into these Elements. At the outset, working through the book may well seem confusing or daunting. You may easily feel overwhelmed chasing some previously elusive goal or navigating emotional life challenges. This is entirely understandable for such a complex intangible subject.

It may be useful to think of the process as like constructing a jigsaw puzzle of yourself in your current place in the Universe. There is a big picture amongst all the pieces contained in the book that will only be revealed with honest self-reflection and repeated practice. On their own each piece offers only a fragment that may hint at a pattern or perhaps sometimes an incoherent picture, rather than revealing the final masterpiece. These pieces of information become gradually clearer and increasingly effective in creating positive change when they are actively applied at the end of each Element and specifically affirmed in chapter six of the book. But in the meantime, as you stretch out your attention and become familiar with each of your jigsaw pieces, their individual shapes and colours, you will start, perhaps imperceptibly, to fit together the pieces and synergise them to reveal the big picture far more powerful than its component parts.

At the end of each Element chapter are three questions for you to reflect on and answer from your own perspective. As you finish each of these chapters, I recommend that you write down in a separate notebook your answers to these questions. These can then be used later in the book to complete the "Big picture".

Like all things that are worth doing well, this is not a process with short cuts, nor is there a final outcome, only a growth of who you can be until your physical self exists no more. Each step is a vital tool to enable you to grow to your maximum potential. I suggest that to create a deeper sense of change and realisation that you re-read each Element and practice the activities several times before moving ahead to the next, so that they become a habitual form of the way you live.

If you are still in doubt about the value of self-examination, a poignant reminder of the failure to try is brought terrifyingly to life in Leo Tolstoy's book "The death of Ivan Illyich." In the book, Ivan, as the title suggests, is at the end of his life and forced to consider the terrible and fearful thought; "What if my whole life has been wrong?" with an increasing certainty that it has been.

Beyond fiction, I am certain that whilst many of us may eventually reach a point of deep contentment, this can be achieved much sooner in our life. It is also unfortunately common for some to never reach this space. If this book helps just one person to avoid being so tormented, or to get to a self-actualised place in a timelier fashion, then it has been worth writing.

◎

Preface.

l started out writing this book with no more than a general notion of pulling together what l considered would be a useful collection of learnings and connections, some obvious, some non-obvious, that will assist in improving mental and subsequently physical well-being, either during many of life's difficulties or through the drive to just become a better version of myself. Snippets of universally beneficial strategies and aspects of humanity that l have learned in my own time in this incarnation. What l hadn't bargained for was the depth to which my own sense of spirituality would blossom and fit centrally and absolutely into my own philosophical, psychological and therapeutic mindset. As l reached the end stages of writing it, l have a contentment and inner peace that l can return to and know at the very deepest level.

As you weave your way through the chapters, there will be two types of motivation that keep you going; negative and / or positive. Negatively you may be struggling in life, or have been thrown some seriously challenging events for which you crave guidance. Positively you may be motivated to grow to become the best version that you can be, deliberately creating your own self as an artist would do in creating a work of art.
Regardless of your own motivation, or indeed your spiritual or non spiritual beliefs, l believe this book offers something for everyone who has a true desire to change, to grow and with an open mind and a love of humanity.

Chapter One
Understanding Ourselves

What we are.

"Have perseverance as one who doth for evermore endure, for thy shadows live and vanish. That which in thee shall live forever, that which in thee knows, for it is knowledge, is not of fleeting life; it is the man that was, that is, and will be, for whom the hour shall never strike."

Helena Blavatsky - The Voice of Silence.

As such complex creatures, how do we make sense of ourselves? Indeed, why do we need to bother? Many don't attempt to, though it seems you are not in this category as you have at least got this far with me. Many don't ever deeply or persistently try, they may loosely dabble in self-examination to varying degrees, but often they become stuck, distracted, bored, fearful, or just too busy. The motivation can be too weak to start, or sometimes too strong and lead to overthinking and confusion. Life itself in all it's hum-drum habitual routines kicks in and deviates us away from giving focus to any process with persistence and consistency to deeply understand ourselves.

Will that be you?

Will it be more important for you to spend an indefinite hour on your social media, tv, virtual reality games, material dreams or repeating chores than to seek the greatest gift you can give yourself; the true wisdom of really, really, really knowing yourself?

But, is there something worthwhile to be gained from what seems like such an arduous task?
Well I believe there are many good reasons to persevere, in fact I could drill down into each and find more within, but for the sake of keeping your attention, I shall list just three of the best reasons to start the ball rolling:

Number one: Freedom from your hidden prison.

You can't let yourself out of prison if you don't know you're in one! Getting to really understand yourself is actually akin to letting yourself out of a prison you didn't know you were in. This is a fundamental reason that also makes it entirely understandable why so many never embark on the journey of self-discovery. As Donald Rumsfeld once famously said;
"Reports that say that something hasn't happened are always interesting to me, because as we know, there are known knowns; there are things we know we know. We also know there are known unknowns; that is to say we know there are some things we do not know. But there are also unknown unknowns; the ones we don't know we don't know." Picking up this book and reading this far would suggest that you are at least open to the fact that there will be unknown unknowns. That in a metaphorical sense, you can see that you are held prisoner to a degree by these unknowns.

Therefore, in regard to your own self-actualisation, you have moved beyond the unknown unknowns stage to the known unknowns stage.

Number two: Your constant growth towards contentment.

You are the most important person in your life and as such, knowing yourself as well as you can, is an amazing opportunity if you want to get the best out of it. You may be thinking that you do know yourself, that you know yourself better than anyone! The second part of that statement may be true, but really knowing ourselves is not quite as simple as we might like to think. For most, if we do happen to learn an important aspect of ourselves, it is almost by accident, for some it is a lifetime's work and for many it doesn't ever really happen, but that doesn't have to be the case. So how often do you question your own beliefs, do you notice and question your automatic thoughts or the hidden functions of your behaviours? You may be able to predict how you think and feel and what you will do, but what are the hidden reasons as to why, and, if you revealed these reasons, could changing your thoughts, feelings and behaviours for the better really happen? Absolutely, this can be achieved and along with that achievement comes a greater comfort and contentment in your Being.

Number three: Your relationships.

Any relationship you have at least comprises

yourself, whether it is the relationship you have with yourself, i.e; your self-worth, self-esteem and self-love, or whether it is the relationship you have with someone else. If you don't have a good understanding of yourself within a relationship, then all your relationships are not only built on rocky ground but to varying degrees are less than genuine, are affected without your control or could perhaps even be called a sham. For this reason alone, we should all be investing ourselves in this task. We will be spending the rest of our lives with ourselves so wouldn't this be the single best investment we could make. In my view, it should be lesson number one in school.

That's just three big reasons why self-examination is important, there are many, many more. What follows is how we understand ourselves.

To start with, it is critical to point out that our Being and the Elements operating within it are what comprises our inner self, and it is here that our subject matter lies. What I mean by our inner selves is our essential nature, not the stories we have grown attached to about ourselves. Tragically these Elements of our inner self are often either not used, used inadequately, or are more typically focused on the outer self and our interactions with the world, from which many of our problems stem. This outer self, in broad strokes, is the huge array of our physical appearances, our statuses, performance and reviews, or indeed our achievements or failures. These in our materialistic, ownership, competitive and image driven world are the part of our self that gets the lions share of both ours and other people's attention. The ego feeds itself on these factors, searching for and gorging itself on status, likes, happy faces and comments. What other people think is to the Ego the only thing that matters. In isolation, there would be nothing wrong with these, but unfortunately, they can't exist in isolation because they are dependant on comparison to others.

Let's not forget, these are outer elements that we typically automatically treat as being more important than our inner self. We also have either zero, or limited control over these temporary outer elements. If we devoted as much time to the inner parts of our self as we do to our outward appearance, materials or status, then individually and consequently the world would be a more peaceful compassionate place. The outer image of self as a success or failure in life is a trap into which our inner self routinely falls. This part of us of course is the Ego which constructs separateness from our fellow beings and from our inner self, degrading the quality of one of our innate needs; that of our relatedness to ourself and others. With a focus on the external, the resulting outer actions of superiority or self-degradation behaviour at either extreme, if left unchecked, become a poison to our inner wellbeing.

Here, we could get bogged down in exploration of the Ego and all its forms and pitfalls, but the current focus is on how we can understand our essential selves, not the Ego, which I suggest is the arch rival to our inner self.

To simplify a little, and for the purpose of this section, I'd like to break ourselves down into four parts;

Our thoughts.
Our feelings.
Our behaviours.
and
Our Being.

I am going to go through the first three here, though Being itself I will leave until the last chapter of the book. Of course, you can flick to the end to read it if your curiosity gets the better of you, but I have addressed this in the final stages of the book for a reason. The experience you get will provide you with a deeper understanding and appreciation of what I mean by Being, therefore having read and implemented the preceding parts to the book, you will be ready to further draw your own sense of Being from this experiential learning.

At this point in our journey together, as you work through reading and practicing each Element, I invite you to simply consider Being as a created space which allows your potentiality, via your Elements, to materialise and flow.

Consider this as an analogy; think of your physical body as a CB radio. If you're too young to know, a CB, or citizens band, radio is a device that allows both receiving and broadcasting of radio signals. It is capable of receiving and transmitting beyond itself. Your Being is like the space in which wavelengths and frequencies can flow, without which the CB radio could not function. The Elements In Being are like the dials which tune the wavelengths and frequencies you receive, as well as the transmitter which broadcasts out in it's chosen wavelengths and frequencies too. Your Elements In Being are tuning in to receive and broadcasting out both internally and externally, creating your inner reality and feeding back to the outer reality. But for the moment, we will leave Being to the side and look to discuss our thinking.

What are our thoughts and where do they come from? Somehow, they form from the specific conglomeration of mysterious synaptic connections firing inside our heads with such rapidity and volume, they could easily resemble the lightening strikes across every planet in every galaxy in the entire known universe.

The human brain is composed of about 100 billion nerve cells. These are a mesh of trillions of interconnected connections, called synapses. Each connection transmits signals that average around one per second, though in some cases, they can reach a rate of up to 1000 signals per second. Amongst the vast array of functions these synaptic firings have are our brains consideration and contemplation of all things and all non-things. That which is real, fantasy speculation and rumination. Incredibly, thought activity can be seen in action under fMRI scans, and indeed research is now working on interpreting dream activity from fMRI brain readouts. But though this is an activity on a micro atomic scale, the ideas, images, memories existing in thoughts are in a non-physical realm.

Being thinkers lead us to beg many questions and philosophise many ideas, including as René Descartes the French philosopher, scientist and mathematician declared "I think therefore I am" or should it perhaps be; I am therefore I think, or alternatively; I am what I think? Of course, I do think, but is that who I am? Or is it just who I think I am?
I prefer to just say "I am" and remember what I believe, and add to those two short words creates my temporary reality. Confused? Keep reading!

In the context of this book, and of understanding ourselves better, when we look at our thinking, a good starting point is to look at thoughts as the processing of information. Our brains are doing this to try and make sense of the world, but they also have a capacity to imagine and reflect, which is nearly always where both our problems start and where our advances are made. Imagination precedes our creativity and our innovation, but it also creates and feeds our fears, monsters and demons. Thinking can expand our learning and understanding, though it can also deteriorate into resistance to what has happened or what may happen, keeping us imprisoned by past trauma and grief or future fears and uncertainties, leading to rumination or regret, worry or anxiety.

Our brains are both amazingly helpful, and yet such torturous devices at the same time. There is also another important factor to consider with thinking, and that is information itself. A good description of information states it as the resolution of uncertainty. The problem here with our resolution of uncertainty is that the perception we have of the world is unique, always changing and often inaccurate. We often make assumptions to resolve uncertainty because it is otherwise too laborious, therefore our information is often falsely certain to us. Changing this comes down to challenging how we look at our thoughts and perceptions, including our reflections.

When we adjust the way we look and think, we adjust the subjects of our observations too. Our world becomes quite different.

The next part of ourselves are our emotional feelings. We might include in this the feelings of our heart and our gut or in our body in general. These parts of us process information too, but they seem to process information in an intuitive way. They are also absolutely connected, instantaneously with the thoughts we have, though often the thoughts that come with our feelings may not easily be articulated, or they may be too painful to consciously bear. Without an acceptance and a rationalisation of the feelings we have, our feelings can then become like a preset guidance system that directs our life without our full control, just like autopilot. This connection between our emotional feelings and thoughts is a two-way street, so what we think in our brain creates emotional feelings in our body and vice versa.

If we are thinking resistantly about how hopeless our circumstances are, of all the bad things that have happened to us, then our emotional feelings will of course be of despair, sadness, fatigue, heaviness and demotivation. As we experience these feelings of emotion, our perception of the world is altered, we become positioned with our eye to a narrow and dark lens of negative focus, and hence our thoughts become negative or hopeless as our perception is skewed. What then occurs is that our feelings create new thoughts formulated from their emotionally driven perspective. Alternatively, we may be thinking gratefully about something in our lives, even if that something is plain or common, and remarkably at times, even if it is less than pleasant, if we can appreciate its' purpose for us, if we can find some form of meaning that it brings, then our emotional connection becomes very different, we can even experience a contentment for things which otherwise would be unacceptable. In this example, as our emotional connection communicates back with the thinking, our thoughts become inline with our emotions and we start to perceive our situation through a different wider lens, a lens that allows more light to pass through and reveals more understanding and opportunity, a lens that grants us the ability to allow what is beyond our control to be.

Thirdly, we have our behaviours, generally these

are the things we physically do, but it is also worth bearing in mind that thinking can become a doing activity as well, particularly when there doesn't feel like any practical activity or process available to us, to do, that will solve a problem. This is particularly prominent when it manifests as worry.

Worry as a behaviour is our way of attempting to solve a problem or resolve some uncertainty and becomes an unhelpful "behaviour" when the problem is persistent and either hypothetical, uncontrollable or beyond our immediate control.

Physical or thinking behaviours then are the third part of what makes us what we are. These behaviours serve as functions, reasons, or as a purpose. We go to the supermarket because we need food, we exercise because we feel physically well from the activity, we play sport because there is a thrill in the competition or a sense of belonging to being part of a team. There is generally more than one function to any of our behaviours, for example we eat to keep us alive, but we may also eat because we enjoy the taste of the food, and unconsciously because we get a hit of dopamine when we have a donut, or because eating may be a social interaction with others.

The fact is though that we do what we do for many reasons. Generally the reasons may be positive, productive and healthily satisfying, but at times of stress, fear, worry, hopelessness and worthlessness, the reasons for our behaviours are often an attempt to avoid, escape from, or block out our feelings and thoughts, but rather than enabling us to work through our thoughts and emotions, they give a temporary relief or escape, only for the problem to re-emerge with greater intensity and a further sense of our own inadequacy in navigating our situation.

One of the most common effects of our patterns of behaviours is to lose our consciousness of the function of that behaviour, whether that be enjoyment gained, relief sought, or reward fulfilled. Upon the first phases of employing a behaviour, there may have initially been a function, however on repetition the consciousness of this function can often be lost as a habit is formed. Habitual behaviour is, in many ways, extremely useful to us as we free up our attention, away from the repetition of frequently undertaken tasks, to other aspects of our world. Observing more fully that there is an instant connection between what we think, feel and do is vital if we are to deepen our own understanding and allow opportunity for change. If we fail to do this, the negative effect can be that we lose our appreciation for the beauty and purpose of our behaviours or drift into distraction, avoidance, withdrawal, compulsion or even addiction without realising.

As an illustration of how these aspects interact, let's take a situational example of the kind of perfect storm that can happen in life. It may or may not sound extreme to you, but as is often the case, one loss often leads to more losses in close succession. Imagine then that you have just lost your job of 15 years, your partner has left you for another person, you are not seeing your children and you see no hope of getting more work anytime soon. This devastating chain of events has, in all likelihood, hijacked your previous patterns of thinking and turned your thoughts to a point where they are entirely dwelling on the losses of your life, the fears of the future, and the errors or wrongs in your work and relationships. This in turn makes you feel, more deeply, the hopelessness of your situation. Like a pit of despair all the negative emotions and demotivation hold you in their grasp. You may think to yourself, what a fool l have been, why didn't l just behave differently? Or the focus may be on the unfairness of the way you have been treated by your boss or the betrayal of your partner? Over time, as these thoughts and feelings build, they may turn inwards to yourself. Thoughts like l am worthless, how is this fair? l am a burden, l am a failure, my partner is better off without me, all start to intrude your mind. These tormenting thoughts and feelings are so weakening to your confidence and character, that blocking them out or shutting yourself away is a seemingly reasonable, natural response. You reduce your interactions, though at the same time crave to be back with your partner, you become angry, sad, consider that it would be better if you were not alive, turn to distractions or substances and this further isolates yourself into your own thinking and your own negative reinforcing behaviour.

This of course is only one example. There are as many variations to this as there are people and circumstances. We all have our own unique blend of traits that guide our default reactions within our particular perceptions, beliefs and situations, but, like creating a map of a strange new land, making sense of your self is still possible and forms the basis, the very foundation for change.

Before moving on to chapter two and to help you to explore further into your thoughts, feelings and behaviours and how they interact, here is an observation plan to work on.

From today, start to pay attention to the three parts of yourself as described above by setting some time aside each day to follow this plan, regardless of whether you are experiencing positive or negative thoughts and feelings.

Stop what you are doing and find a place where you can sit quietly. Being outside and in a natural environment works best if possible. At this point, I want you to imagine that you are observing yourself from above, as if from the far corner of the ceiling or hovering 2 meters above yourself. Watch your physical body experiencing the feelings you are having in this moment. Start to pay attention to how you are feeling in this moment. Content? Restless? Peaceful? Sad? Nervous? Irritable? Edgy? Worried?

Notice what thoughts are coming along with those feelings, there may be questioning or judging thoughts, predictions or frustrations. All these thoughts are simply part of, and at the same time, feeding the emotion you are feeling.

Regardless of whether they are positive or negative, allow them to be as they are, just in this moment.

Now consider what you would normally be doing or would like to do. There is no need to do this, but just observe the thought and desire you have, as again, coming from the feelings and thoughts. Again, allow this to be.

Once you start to feel more comfortable with observing your own thoughts and feelings, refocus your attention on what else you notice about the moment you are in. The sounds, the sights, people, buildings, plants, sky. The temperature, the wind. What you sense physically, your feet connected with the ground, your clothes against your skin. Your breath coming into and leaving your lungs. Ask yourself who is witnessing this moment? Notice yourself as the perceiver without which this moment would not exist.
Once you feel deeply calm and connected with your surroundings and the moment, continue with your day.

To increase the benefit of this process, make a commitment to deliberately do this when you are feeling stressed, worried or anxious.

Do this several times over the next few days, re-reading this chapter before moving on to the next part.

Chapter Two
The Hub

Element One : Reflection

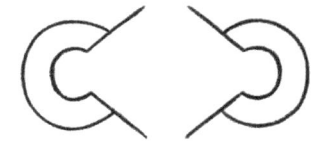

"The unexamined life isn't worth living."
Socrates

In many ways I chose the word Element, as the descriptor and title in this book, because the aspects of being human are like substances created from the chemical elements of the periodic table, they are the building blocks of who we are. However, they are infinitely more complex in their interdependence and influence on each other, so defining them as singular and pure is in reality virtually impossible. As this is the case, any order in which they are presented is not intended as a hierarchy, though, I have deliberately chosen to focus first on the Elements of Reflection and Attention (in the present moment). My reasons for this are to illustrate how absolutely integral good Reflection and Attention are to every other

Element and how in a real sense they form the hub of the wheel on which the other elements turn.

As we proceed with the first Element, what is meant by Reflection?

Well, if you are to embark on a process of long term, rather than temporary change, an ability to continuously, openly and honestly reflect on yourself, and what has happened, is necessary. As humans, our reflective capacity is one of the fundamental differences between us and the other species. Good Reflection creates self-guided discovery. It is your ability to review an experience openly and honestly from within yourself. It has the purpose of improving your learning or understanding, to effect positive change for the future and to manage uncertainty. It pulls together your current level of understanding surrounding an experience and tests how congruent your thoughts, feelings and behaviours were at the time of an event, compared to that of your current understanding. Inevitably, if Reflection is done well, then you will not only identify areas for growth, learning and change, but you will process, clarify and challenge your understanding, rehearse a change for the future, and be ready to activate growth as more and more future opportunities become clearer in your awareness.

In actively commencing this kind of Reflection, there is also a hidden dilemma. Good Reflection is challenging and requires seeing through a more "removed" perspective. Think of the abhorrent feelings evoked in the disfigured patient who avoids revealing the hideous scars beneath the bandages on their body. Because reflecting on the negative self is so challenging and often uncomfortable, you will have become well versed in avoiding it. That is to say, challenges can lead to behaviours, thought patterns, and habits of avoidance that repeat without an awareness of their underlying function. This habit then, is in effect a path of least resistance that provides immediate comfort, but not always positive change or growth. I'm not criticising here, I can be as guilty as the next person in being drawn unaware into avoidant or distraction behaviour, because reviewing yourself can be a very uncomfortable and a seemingly counter productive experience. Not only that, but reflecting takes deliberate effort, time and perseverance. Why would we want to reflect carefully and in detail about something that we did less than well? Our own little self feels under threat from such critique and these reflections can evoke feelings of angst, shame, guilt or low-self esteem, particularly if reflection is done with judgement and a lack of openness.

When reflecting, our thoughts will be driven by how we feel. Maybe we will feel that we were not at fault, that the situation conspired against us. Perhaps we lost our temper with the kids or our partner, maybe we drank too much last night for the third night in a row. Looking back in a reflective way on this is not somewhere most will want to go and indeed requires a deliberate shifting of perspective. What's the point in torturing ourselves by looking at what we did "wrong" and how do we even see this from an unbiased third person perspective?

Let me just say at this point that I'm using the word "wrong" through gritted teeth. It is not helpful to us when we judge. Rarely do we impartially contextualise a situation, and acknowledge what is wrong, with enough depth and perspective to see that it is all that could rationally occur given all the circumstances in which it has happened. When we genuinely reflect on the judging behaviour of either ourselves or another, we must ask ourselves; given the sum of life circumstances and experience, that I and / or the other person has, could we honestly expect a different behaviour? By reflecting in this way, we not only have an opportunity to change, but we acknowledge our feelings, so that rather than being a hidden feeling which quietly, secretly manipulates our behaviour, we do four very important things:

1. Rationalise what we have done.
2. Be compassionate to ourselves.
3. Break free from our own repeating storyline.
4. Test out alternative options.

Avoidance behaviours become our path of least resistance and place a barrier to achieving any depth of reflection. Because of this, a default, habitual type of negative thinking tends to happen that is focused externally on an event or another person or group. You may think to yourself how badly you have been treated, or how unlucky you are, or of somebody or something that was "wrong". You may be absolutely justified in the feelings you have attached to these thoughts. Disrespect, bullying, harassment and violence, in all its forms are scourges of humanity's Ego, yet though we may not have control over others behaviour, with practice and reflection we can have control of our own responses, and subsequently determine our own destiny.

Each day there could be dozens of occasions when you feel wronged, where you are offended. Let's be honest here, this is one thing you can be sure of in life! Things do go wrong, people will offend you. It's not unreasonable to feel aggrieved when you have been wronged or things haven't gone your way, BUT..... in being caught in this kind of focus, it is easy to lose your ability to reflect with clarity on yourself AND.... you lose the chance to change what is directly in your control; your attitude to the situation, and a good perspective. In this situation you pass all ownership of a problem to somebody or something else, and if you don't own it, guess what? You can't change it. You have to wait for someone else or something else to change. You could and probably will be waiting forever for that to happen.

But shouldn't I be mad? It's good to get it out isn't it? Or isn't it just better to completely avoid reflecting, or thinking about what I can't change? I'll just keep busy, get drunk, gamble, hit the drugs, and block it out... it will pass won't it? Why must I focus on myself when this thing that just happened isn't right, just or fair? Sure, you can do that if you want.... Keep being mad, rail against the injustice in your own mind if you want.... Keep the suffering alive because that is what you are doing. However, now is when you will let go of it, whether that now is in the next hour, day, week, month, year, decade or at the end of your life, at some point in a future now, you will let go of it. If not now, then when?

Now is always the time to let go of the suffering you maintain in yourself, and is also, as will be reinforced later, maintained via those that you share your life with.

The reality is that each one of us will do only what we are able to do at any given time based on our level of Reflection and consciousness. If you do not focus on yourself, then you are not yet ready, and therefore what is perpetuated is your own suffering.

The first noble truth Buddha tells us is; Life is suffering. As with so many of the situations we become trapped in, there can be a profound paradox. In this situation when we reflect well then, we may accept the suffering that is beyond our control, and then act to change for the better that which is in our control, thereby alleviating the suffering. The alternative and paradox is that reflecting with a resistance to the suffering, or avoiding it altogether seems correct because suffering is bad, but all that does is perpetuate it.

In his Auguries of Innocence, William Blake used

the metaphor of the reflective light from the Sun by the Moon to remind us of the power of Reflection and the uncertainty that transpires without it:

> *"If the Sun & Moon should doubt*
> *They'd immediately go out."*

Complexity and distraction are huge barriers to good Reflection, and our world is absolutely rife with both easy distraction and endless complexity. Living in the digital information age of the internet, tv, social media and mass communication provides a constant pull away from reflection and into distraction. This is an information rich environment in which we can be constantly connected, switched on, and increasingly addicted to distractive thinking. The problem here is the effect it has on our attention, we only have a limited capacity of attention, and the more technology and information grows, the shorter our attention becomes. As the information we receive increases and becomes more insidious, our attention is spread more thinly across it. So much to take in and so little time to focus. This modus operandi is developing rapidly and as we know from neuro-plasticity, repetitive processing styles set up and reform the connective pathways of our brains. Like anything, if we do the same thing over and over again, it becomes a default, habitual behaviour with a strong neural pathway.

We think without thinking, and if we think without thinking, who is flying the plane.....Autopilot?

Who is flying your plane?

Let us now work through an example of how you might use positive reflective practice.

Imagine that you have caught yourself in rumination about how you were not respected, treated appropriately, or perhaps let down by a friend, colleague or loved one.

The chances are that you feel upset, angry or disappointed, you may be saying to yourself:
"Why did they do that"?
"Couldn't they just respect me"?
"How would they feel if I did that to them"?

With reflective practice and courage, it is never too late to start. You may have been travelling mentally down a negative reflective path for sometime, but it only takes a moment to realise, and once you notice this, you have an opportunity to change how you reflect.

In a few steps, here is what we can do:

Step One.
Don't tune out, tune in.

Your first step in Reflection is to revisit a situation or difficult encounter with a kind of observing eye on yourself, as if you are a spectator looking down upon your own experience. As you do this, picture in your minds eye the place and situation in as much detail as possible.
Now, notice your feelings as you participated in the event, rather than unconsciously churning over

emotive feelings, ask yourself:
What thought is attached to that feeling?
What is the feeling trying to say?

When reflecting well on a situation, we will be focusing on our own responses to the situation as much as to the situation itself. What did the situation cause in me? How are my responses (thoughts, feelings, emotions and behaviours) preventing me from moving past this, or how did they influence what took place?

These are often the missing questions. In a situation void of good reflection, the focus of our thinking is on the outer circumstances, and often has a sense of judgement and resistance, but rarely focuses on the resistance itself that comprises our inner thoughts, feelings and subsequent behaviours.

Once there is an observing eye on our inner perspective included in our reflections we can move to the next step.

Step Two
Acknowledge it for what it is – no judgement needed.

Here we can now start to acknowledge our own responses based on our level of consciousness.
Our level of consciousness is different at this moment of Reflection to the original time of the event, because we are deliberately taking the time to consider the many dimensions of an event, and

are not as directly emotionally affected by the event itself. We can also see more clearly the parts of what occurred at the time that were outside of our control.

Do you have direct control of how others respect you, judge you or understand you? What is in your control, what is outside your control?
What can you have influence on by the way you are?

Step Three
Rationalise.

Now we have reflected on our own responses and acknowledged them completely, we are ready to rationalise what has happened. As in this case, another person is involved that has added to your path of negative thinking, because we are looking at the situation with a certain distance, we can begin to understand that they could only operate from their level of consciousness at that time. This is all any of us can do. If they were able to reflect well then, they would have been able to see how they weren't respecting you, and may then have chosen a different action. On the other hand, there may also be things about yourself that you can change. Perhaps you have had previous bad experiences in which you were disrespected. Underlying, you may unintentionally have a weak spot that makes you more emotionally vulnerable to feeling let down. If you become conscious through reflection of this, then you can rationalise your response and create an opportunity to recognise this the next time you feel disrespected. There is a very real shift in your sense of empowerment and ability to control yourself when you examine your life in this way. Socrates was spot on!

To reiterate then, at challenging times Reflection is the most difficult yet offers the greatest learning opportunity, particularly when it is less than pleasant, or going against the grain of your current emotion. When you repeatedly practice reflecting in this way, you will become less fearful of failure, as you start to see that failure is only real when you don't learn from it. With practice and the positive reinforcement from your increased sense of control, your changed reflective style will become a new default.

"Even the most courageous among us only rarely has the courage to face what he already knows."
Friedrich Nietzsche

Good Reflection requires a high degree of calmness, peace and acceptance. During periods of anxiety, stress or depression, when being able to reflect is most important, it is paradoxically the most difficult. This is because when you are anxious or depressed, your view of the world and yourself is distorted through fear, hopelessness, and a magnified view of potential dangers. To start to address this, as we move through each step of our reflective practice, we must pay particular attention to our anxieties and mood, which typically increases the degree of our negative questioning, shameful, critical and judgemental focus both in thoughts and feelings. As we observe ourselves, and notice these key anxious or depressed traits, we can rationalise them, and begin to accept them for what they are at that time. They are just part of our anxiety, our fear, our mood and despite their, sometimes horrific nature, it is ok that they occur. It just means we are human.

A major benefit of reflecting with a non-judgemental, accepting frame of mind is that it allows you to work on issues rather than to deny, resist or push them aside. Through this non-judgemental and accepting lens, you can reflect effectively, you can look clearly, unashamedly, and honestly at the entirety of what has occurred.

Reflection is a challenging process, particularly when you feel you are not "hitting the mark" and it is most difficult when you start out. Sometimes you are paying attention to things you have previously avoided, masked, hidden or denied for the very first time. With your current level of consciousness, you may well not think that there lies any hidden understanding of yourself worthy of challenge and change. But let me assure you there will be and indeed this can be confronting. No one operates without some habitual behaviour so it is vital to acknowledge that this is not an easy task. Yet it is one that is essential and as with all tasks, one that becomes easier as it is practiced.

As reflection becomes easier and if it is maintained,

it can move from being a post event state of mind, to an in event state of consciousness, a kind of reflective attention. This is usually a very gradual transition, often flitting between being achievable, and not as circumstances vary in the degree to which they are challenging, thus, sometimes allowing or preventing in event reflection. Knowing this, it is useful to give ourselves permission that it's OK to not always achieve what we set out to do, that we aren't failing, just learning and practicing.

Before moving to our next hub Element, I shall mention at this point the common occurrence of drift, which if you allow it, will derail your complete progress. This is applicable to all the Elements in Being, but it is worthy of mention here at the outset. This drift, or derailment, often occurs because there is always a tendency to return to previous habitual behaviours or thinking styles during the practice of any new skill. The old patterns we have are deeply and structurally embedded in our brains and our personality. They will be waiting silently, stealthily in the wings to reactivate, even when you have practiced long and hard. This is why practice is so important. Simply reading the book is unfortunately not enough.

Each additional Element when practiced will provide more evidence of the value of your continued efforts. To keep yourself motivated and incentivised, be clear now about your intentions. Whether they are to be the best version of yourself or to overcome your fears worries or anxieties.

Write them down now on your fridge or bathroom mirror to remind yourself of your beautiful intention, preventing drift and keeping you going even when the going gets tough.
Good Reflection is a preventer for drift

Finally. Take a moment now to consider some Reflections and then write them down:

1. What is one key realisation or reinforcement of your own knowledge of Reflection that you can take away from this chapter?
2. What could you improve on in your use of the Element of Reflection?
3. What do you do well in your use of the Element of Reflection?

Element Two : Attention
(in the present moment)

This garnished path quietly beckons,
A gentle stroll through scented woods,
Skin bathed in beams of dappled light,
Emerge, immersed in brilliant white.
Gone! No more sick ravaged dread,
As each attentive step I tread,
Halts the hand of ticking clock,
I am as tree, and sky and rock.
Weave and thread through golden meadow,
Remaining high by keeping low.
Descending down to silver stream.
This is all an infinite dream.
Now stop quietly, to sit and listen,
And be a while and listen.

In the previous chapter I discussed Reflective practice and the importance of it as one of the Elements in the hub to which all the other Elements connect. Paying Attention or being aware in the present moment feeds directly into Reflective practice, and is the second component at the centre, and without doubt the strongest Element. If you are not aware of something, if you don't give it your attention, then you have a common and serious handicap to life. It may seem glaringly obvious but sometimes, for the sleepwalkers amongst us, it is necessary to point the conspicuous out.

However, there is a reason that we stop paying attention, so don't think it's a fault. Losing attention is something that we do in many ways by design. Paying attention takes up a lot of time and processing power, and therefore means it can feel like a tedious process, and a brake to other tasks. What we do all the time is learn, through attention behaviours, processes and thinking. We repeat a thought or action with ever decreasing conscious attention, until our learning enters our subconscious where it then becomes a default or habit. Now at this stage we no longer have to pay attention to it, we can free up our attention to other things and in the background have our subconscious run the show. We can all think of examples of this, like driving somewhere and not recalling how we got there, or when we are reading and get to the end of the paragraph or page and find Attention has been lost, yet we were still reading the words before us.

As I discussed earlier, this is a bigger problem than it previously was now that we inhabit a world of high-speed living, a continual lack of time, of continuous information, striving and competing, of deadlines and targets, of increasing clutter and responsibilities. The opportunity to pay good attention to our environment, to ourselves, and to become aware of our inner thoughts and feelings can, and often is, essentially eroded to the point where we are no longer human beings, but rather humans being done. The interjection, at every moment of our modern lives, of data, screen time and mobile communication, is resulting in a habitual pattern of thinking which is disconnected from and yet infecting the purity of our Attention.

For clarity at this point, what I mean by the purity of our Attention is the focus of our awareness on the here and now, to the exclusion of people, places, times or things that are not in our presence. We must pay attention to our thoughts as they occur in the present moment, but acknowledge that they are just thoughts. At its greatest level, the purity of our Attention also has an overarching awareness of it's own Attention. Attention and thinking then are very different but in the way we generally function they are not differentiated. Thinking infects and distracts our Attention constantly, therefore to be able to separate out our Attention from our thinking, and to practice having a purity to it brings enormous benefit to every aspect of our well-being.

The 21st century world is rife with mental health challenges, not least because our thinking and attention are disastrously overloaded and intertwined. We are bombarded with a plethora of options and choices, through a multitude of interfaces, not just in the physical world but through all our electronic devices; what clothes to wear, food to consume, friend to befriend, friend to unfriend, phone plan to choose, specification of car to opt for. The list goes on and on. These are all infiltrating and forming the existence of our present moments through our Attention. This is our reality, so if we are to be purely present in our Attention, then it must be within our physical perceptual vicinity, not a representation of someone or something beyond the here and now, not a thought projection of things beyond where you are in time and space.

Of course, achieving complete purity in your present moment is nigh on impossible without practice, at least for any length of time. Consciousness of the present is the degree to which you are able to notice the thoughts which you are bringing into the present, yet are not part of your perceptual vicinity. Noticing this allows us to acknowledge the infection of the purity of our Attention, and then take conscious control by refocusing on what exists in our present moment. If for example, we were to go for a slow meandering walk through a park, gaze at the trees and birds, listen to the sounds of the insects buzzing, and feel the warm breeze against our skin and then hear our phone ping, we could say our presence has a high degree of purity. But then as we look at the images and information on our phone, our purity of presence is degraded. Our thinking has moved away from now focus into a disconnected territory. In a real sense the phone and its communication are like your own thoughts and has become them. But they are not real as such, they are an expression or representation of what may be real or imagined by another person, or an artificial intelligence, and now you. They exist in an invisible space, are not your here and now, yet they have become your here and now by hijacking your attention away from the purity of your present moment.

At this point I would like to highlight one of our other Elements In Being that will be enhanced through improving our Attention. The kind of thinking I have been discussing here that is disrupting our Attention is also fencing in and prohibiting our important, inherent, spontaneous creativity journeys, or what is described later as our Element of Dreaming.

Relearning and re-engaging in the art of becoming aware and attending to ourselves in the modern environment, is more often than not, a battle because we are competing for attention with so many (seemingly more important) things, as well as challenging our default thinking processes. But, remember, as with all the other Elements, without this skill, we will always be in the slow lane to change, we will always have a barrier to appreciation, we will always have a disconnect from happiness. We will always, as I have found increasingly true, have a disconnection from creativity. Why a slow lane to change, a barrier to appreciation and a disconnection from happiness??? Because, though we may pursue these in our lives, to experience or affect them, they must ensue. They must be attended to in the here and now. Now is all there is and all there ever will be.

I'm pretty sure that virtually every reader will be challenged at times by having to deliberately pay attention with a fully present focus, and without this quickly degrading as the moments tick by. I know I am. Preventing drift away from this purposeful attention and into the pull of thought, the distraction of the presence of information, and the demands of time constraints, is for most virtually impossible for any reasonable length of time. As we grow up, movement out of infancy and childhood sees a progressive loss of the natural ability and ease of non-judgemental attention. Anyone observing the average young child will see a quality of focus on the present that, compared to an adult, is exceptional in its detail. We can also see that this is accompanied with a different relationship to time, a relationship that again deteriorates, as well as speeds up, as we get older. As older children and adults we have lost the natural ability to be comfortable in just being, and without enquiring thought beyond the now.

Thought continuously pulls our attention away from what is, into what might be or what was, or into why and how, and along with this our sense of time speeds up creating more disconnection from right now.

You may be realising there is an importance I hold,

and a seemingly masochistic delight in the challenging. If you are, then you would indeed be partially correct! Not that I enjoy the infliction of pain, but I know that a challenge is like a huge flashing neon sign pointing you to a direction of positive change. Real, meaningful change requires moving into new territory, often unchartered, scary spaces. These changes are also challenging because they are opposite to the normal default path you take. They seem paradoxical in nature, something that you will start noticing is a strong theme in this book, as well as through life.

I want you to keep this in the front of your mind as you move through each Element: The paradox and the challenge.

Embrace the challenges: They are actually gifts bringing opportunities.

Embrace the paradox: They are confirmation of the nature of the Universe. Notice that in so many cases, it is the opposite course of action taken that brings you the effect you desire. So, if it's challenging to you, then this is the indicator that you are moving into real change, not simply skirting around the edge of old patterns. This is true for everyone, and so becoming aware of how this affects others as well, will be of great value in understanding and rationalising their behaviours and road blocks. Unfortunately, simply pointing this out to someone else is not sufficient to create change. Anyone wishing to make this challenging shift must have access to their own Elements in

Being in order to push through the fear of the unknown and make change arise; that has to be worthy of action.

Now that I have established some of the factors that make paying attention or awareness in the present moment so challenging, let me point to the act itself. Firstly, it needs to be a deliberate act. Setting out with a clear plan of the how's, why's and where's will keep you in the attention game. Next it is best to start with short time frames and relaxed or slow activities. Remember, our sense of urgency and time is a barrier to good Attention so slowing down is good. I get it that when I say slow activities, this in itself can be difficult for a lot of people. The fact is that if you are stressed or anxious, you will have a sense of being time poor, or of greater immediacy, your thoughts will be quicker, your voice louder and faster and your pace elevated. The problem here is that the faster we go, the faster we think and then the less we can pay attention to.

As an example of how things could be changed down, if your plan is to use a walk while paying attention then halve your normal walking speed, unless you are a particularly slow walker. Or if you are doing it while eating use smaller portions, and take smaller mouthfuls, chewing at half pace. Give yourself permission here in feeling ok to struggle somewhat.

As I keep saying, this is challenging work, so you want to make it easy for yourself and avoid setting a goal that is too hard, which will only create a feeling of failure if you don't make it. In the early stages of doing this, busy, stressed or anxious people will often feel frustrated by the pace at which they have to go. It is not unusual to say to oneself at these times, "what a waste of time, why am I even doing this when I could (or should) be doing something 'more' important?" But I want you to hear this internal conversation, and challenge it by testing it with your slow behaviour. Pay Attention to it! Come on, we're only talking about a few minutes here. What have you got to lose?

It's not unreasonable to start with just a few seconds, say 20 or 30 seconds, or perhaps 2 or 3 minutes. Choose a period when you are feeling less time poor, when you are at your most alert and undistracted, and where you can get away, if possible, from sterile, busy and thought stimulating man made environments and into natural ones. As your practice increases, you will be able to increase the time spent deliberately paying present moment attention, as well as eventually increasing your ability to do this in more distractive and stressful situations.

Some big questions here are:
What you are paying attention to? And,
how are you paying attention to it?

To answer these questions, it is best if we use an example. Let us picture a place and time where you have deliberately set out to practice your attention to the present moment. Imagine you are spending

10 minutes near some open water, perhaps a lake in a park. What do you notice in your presence? The sunlight glistening on the water, warming the feathers of the ducklings paddling furiously toward the bread that a young boy in a red woollen cable knitted jumper has thrown in the water. The sun warms your skin too, and assists the green paint to peel off the bench where you sit as you notice the synchronicity between all that comprises the moment, including yourself. Then also you notice that you are the perceiver of the moment. It is your individual perception of it that brings it uniquely to life.

So, though you are not orchestrating the moment you are giving it meaning and existence and are integral to it. Fully being present in it. Taking in the moment may be likened to the poet writing a poem with a reverence for what is.

Remember, what may come to be part of the moment, or in a sense infect the present, is a diversion of thinking towards another place or time. Thinking outside of the present is never, if ever far away. It's in our DNA to forecast, plan and reflect. This is what has ensured our survival and allowed us to "advance". But where we have thoughts about another time or place, we are effectively bringing that other time in to this present one. We have at this point become lost outside of the present.

As this happens, you may notice your mind drifts to the problems of the day, the potential trouble ahead, your bank account, your soured relationships, global warming, what you have to do when you get home, your own self-doubts, worries or fears. These thoughts might be trivial or they might be deeply troubling, but what they are is a disconnection from right now. They are infecting what is otherwise a time or place which is 100% real, 100% a part of you, 100% known, 100% existential.

How you pay attention is with non-judgement, acceptance, and with a deep awareness of the interconnectedness of all things.
For example, let's go back to our scene by the lake. There are an almost infinite number of aspects to attend to in this moment, but you can start by breaking them down into categories.

There are the external sensory aspects. Those that are external to yourself, which you can experience with your senses. Here we need to use a 360-degree perspective.
This can be enhanced by using your peripheral vision, as well as your centrally focused visual perspective. Become aware with a peripheral sense, as this is less clouded with the thinking labelling mind, and grounded in the abstract and universal sense of what is. Notice the multiplicity around you from the clouds moving in the sky above, to the fine downy feathers on the paddling ducks causing ripples on the water in front of you, to the ants searching the bench underneath where you sit for tiny crumbs of the previous occupant who ate their lunchtime sandwich. The leaves in

the tree above fluttering in the breeze. The smells of the grass, the summer air or your fading cologne. The sounds of the water, the distant traffic, the air leaving your lungs and rising to blend with the clouds. Feel the bench beneath your legs and the warmth of the sun on your skin. In your awareness of all these aspects, notice also how they are connected to, affect and influence one another, including yourself.

This is so important I am going to say it again:
In your awareness of all these aspects, notice also everything is ultimately connected to, affecting and influencing one another, including yourself.

Notice then the internal sensory aspects of the moment. Tune into the feelings in your body, can you feel the tension in your muscles or have they gone relaxed? Do you feel a sense of peace or a sense of restlessness? Are you hungry, thirsty, happy, content or sad? Pay attention to how you are part of this moment and connected with everything else in it. Your breath is the air that helps move the leaves and caresses the flowers that spread the scent to the bees to pollinate. The connections are endless, and these are only the ones available to your awareness.

Next, pay attention to your own thoughts. They are manifesting for you, what this moment is. Are those thoughts of here and now or, as previously discussed, have you brought in from beyond this moment a different place or time, infecting what is present with what is not?

Of course, thinking beyond the present moment or present space is necessary for many reasons. You need to plan your meals, your work, your future. You can learn from reflecting on the past. But it is not necessary in this chosen moment. How often is your thinking disconnecting you from the most important time that you can experience; the present moment.

The Element of Attention, in the present moment is essentially known to most as mindfulness. There is a fashionable popularity for mindfulness at present, and in general this to me is a heartening situation, but the unnecessary downside I see, is the branding of what is a deliberate state of consciousness into a kind of activity that requires set patterns and processes. One that may leave the impression to practitioners that mindfulness requires more process intervention than it actually needs. This is excellent to assist people to get started, but is not entirely necessary, in fact it can become a crutch on which you may become dependent, like an App or a Group class, and prevent real discipline. Not that intrinsically there is anything wrong with either, but that you can practice your Attention in the present moment anywhere, at anytime, with or without anyone, and the more independently you can practice this without aids, the more variety in attention you will bring, the more openness to connections you will create and the more skilled you will become with your Element of Attention.

Final reflection. Using your Element of Attention

requires putting yourself in a timeless state. To help with this imagine, as hard as it is, that there is no time. When you have finished reading this sentence, put the book down, stop and then consider a state where timelessness is real. No tasks to do, no deadlines to meet, no goals beyond. This moment is the goal. It doesn't matter what you do, or don't do. There is simply nothing more important than right now. There can't be because right now is all you have. What does this feel like for you?

Now take a moment to consider some Reflections and then write these down:

1. What is one key realisation or reinforcement of your own knowledge of Attention that you can take away from this part?
2. What could you improve on in your use of the Element of Attention?
3. What have you done well in your use of the Element of Attention?

Chapter Three
The Space In-between

Element Three : Dreaming

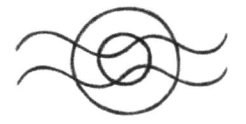

"The greatest achievement was at first and for a time a dream. The oak sleeps in the acorn; the bird sleeps in the egg; and in the highest vision of the soul, a waking angel stirs. Dreams are the seedlings of realities."

James Allen – Author and Poet

Dreaming...

In a sense, dreaming is quite opposite to the hub Elements of Reflection and Attention in the way it acts. The deliberateness of activating it consists of doing nothing, rather than doing something. It requires space. Space from doing and from thinking. To illustrate this, we can see in the quote above from James Allen what the source of the

Element of Dreaming is. It sleeps like the oak in the acorn, like the bird in the egg. It is the still potential that lies waiting to be accessed and when our mind is entirely undistracted and in unity with our heart, when it is in the "highest vision of the soul", the potential can be realised as the "waking angel stirs".

As we look at the Element of Dreaming, we can see that it is infinitely more than something that happens when your consciousness switches off. Indeed, in a very real sense, it is itself infinite.
It is beyond a kind of fantasy that you wish you were living, and at its very core is an access to finding potentiality, ironically beyond your wildest dreams!

What I'm getting at here with the Element of Dreaming, is the allowance of a mental state of freedom to create and to manifest. To allow an access to what is without, and to let surface what is within that cannot be otherwise seen with the clouded, active and distracted mind and body.

Dreaming, whether during sleep or wake, is a time when we must be un-encumbered by the restrictions of the material physical world. All things must be possible. Very much in the way Tilopa expressed over 1000 years ago, we must;
"Have a mind that is open to everything and attached to nothing".

Though Tilopa may not have been referring specifically to the dream state, he describes what is essential and necessary in it. To dream is to allow spontaneous creation with openness, timelessness, and without restrictions of the physical.

We might liken this to an artist, a creator of something from nothing. The artist must first have a blank canvas. An emptiness that is underlying and eternal. Then we have our experiences and imagination, like the oils for the canvas, in all their colours and textures we paint our pictures in dreams.

In a sense this seems similar to the Aboriginal Dreaming, or the beginning of knowledge. It may also be likened to the analogy of the vase and the space within it. Here, what matters is the empty space that allows the water to be held, not the vase itself or the material from which the vase is made. The importance of this space is absolute. If we extend the analogy to the creation of the entire Universe, we can see that it is impossible for the Big Bang to occur without the emptiness in which it was formed.

Our dreaming is a creator like an architect draws their plan. Like the source, nature, god or the divine, the architect forms a blueprint, a potential of material existence or physical action that comes from a place of the metaphysical.

But how do you access your dreams and then use them to build from their blueprint?

First, we must believe and understand the power

of them; returning to Tilopa's wise words: we must be open to them, to everything, yet not attached to them. If we are open to their creative power, to the way in which they allow non-obvious connections to occur because of their lack of rules and barriers, then we piece together new manifestations beyond our wake bound perspective. If we are also unattached to them, our consciousness does not become an inhibitor to further creation, as the wake bound perspective attempts to take control once more if their appearance be less than imagined or does not occur.

Secondly, we must prepare ourselves for lucid dreaming in order to take greater advantage of the dreams creative power. Lucid dreaming is the state of consciousness, in which we are aware that we are dreaming, and have the ability to engage consciously in the dream. Imagine being able to ask a character in your dream, to paint you a masterpiece, or write you a poem. Imagine dreaming the perfect melody and lyrics, and then remembering them when you wake. Anecdotally, many famous creative pieces have manifested from the dreamscape. Paul McCartney's "Yesterday" and "Let it be". Keith Richards "Satisfaction".

The access to create connections not otherwise seen is found in yet further examples, such as with Niels Bohr, the father of quantum mechanics who was said to have had an inspirational dream that subsequently led to his discovery of the structure of the atom. Albert Einstein's principle of relativity also came to him in a dream.

I suggest to you that dreaming, whether day dreaming or night dreaming, is an access point to a hidden intelligence, opening a door to the creation of blueprints, ideas and connections which are, in other levels of consciousness, hidden or clouded. It is easy to dismiss dreaming's importance. The insecurity, caused by relinquishing the control of our conscious brain to this greater unknown, may for some be like an admission of their own limitations of intelligence, as well as that of being able to accept an unseen, intangible, overarching, infinite and universal consciousness.

Lucid dreaming is one description of entering this access point. Lucid dreaming is about gaining intelligible and comprehensible access. Dreaming in this way is then more understandable and coherent. But how do you dream like this?

The paradox here is that it requires a consciousness of the unconscious. There are obviously overlaps between the two, after all this is why we can sometimes remember our unconscious dreams in our conscious state, and it is not uncommon to experience having a dream, and then returning to it with a consciousness which influences and guides the dreams path. The access point then, comes from our awareness that we are dreaming, and then a deliberate participation in it.

There is a simple way to achieve this during sleep, dreaming by using a cue. This is a specific action that you have decided upon and should be reinforced with repetition. One of the most common cues is to be conscious of the palms of your hands. Before you sleep look closely at the palms of your hands and tell yourself that as you see them in your dream, you will become aware of the dream and have the ability to involve your conscious in it.

Another important action to take is to set specific times in your day to ask your self "Am I dreaming?" and include in this schedule a final statement to yourself: "In my dreams tonight, I will be a witness and participant". Not everyone will get to grips with this immediately, but with persistence and practice you will find the best cue for you, and become more "active" in your dreams.

When we consider the unknown, unfathomable aspects of Dreaming it is no wonder that it is dismissed by many as an inconsequential or even meaningless activity. The following words, which were also borrowed by US presidential candidate Robert Kennedy in his 1968 election campaign, I believe illustrate the crucial option we all have when it comes to our dreaming, that of being closed or open;

"We dream about things that never were and say: why?
But I dream things that never were and I say: Why not?"
George Bernard Shaw.

William Shakespeare went much deeper suggesting that dreams are the formation of ourselves within our material existence and time and perhaps beyond, in the form of Creation;

"We are such stuff as dreams are made on; and our little life is rounded with a sleep."
The Tempest

Within Australian Aboriginal culture, many consider the Dreaming or "Dreamtime" is the understanding of the world, of its creation, and its great stories. The Dreaming is the beginning of knowledge, from which came the laws of existence. For survival these laws must be observed.

Like all your Elements In Being, understanding is only part of the journey, awareness of your understanding as you move through life, must follow along with the deliberate and genuine application of this understanding, and finally, reflection on your application. Illustrating this in his book "Walden", Henry David Thoreau stated his own knowing of how dreams can work for us all;

"If one advances confidently in the direction of his dreams, and endeavors to live the life which he has imagined, he will meet with a success unexpected in common hours."

Consider the creative and inspired ideas, work or art that you have been open enough to manifest from within. Did these occur at that quiet time, semi awake in the middle of the night, or perhaps, when your mind was free to wander as you tended the garden or gazed idly through the train or bus window on your commute to work?

Consider also that what you created occurred because you had the space of unrestricted access to it.

Without seeking, it was found.
Without looking, it appeared.
Without distraction and in space, it became yours.

Have patience that dreaming will manifest special gifts, just like the patience nature's dreaming has with itself:

"Consider the lilies of the field, how they grow; they neither toil nor spin, yet I tell you, even Solomon in all his glory was not arrayed like one of these."
Mathew 6: 25-33.

Starting today, set specific time aside to be still and quiet. Put your attention deep within, but do not wait with expectation for miraculous appearances. Notice only that you are the miraculous appearance in this moment. You are the I am, without an attachment or definitions such as I am tired, I am bored, I am happy, I am sick. Just be the I am and from this place languish in its space. Here, if you allow them your dreams will be created in all their glory.

Become the power of your dreaming, and advance confidently towards them, allowing the manifestation of what you dream to become your material reality, remember, always underlying all that is material is the dream.

Finally. Take a moment to consider some Reflections and then write these down:

1. What is one key realisation or reinforcement of your own experience of Dreaming that you can take away from this chapter?
2. What could you improve on in your use of the Element of Dreaming?
3. What have you done well in your use of the Element of Dreaming?

Chapter Four
The Wheel Rim

Element Four : Connection

"The fountains mingle with the river
And the rivers with the ocean,
The winds of heaven mix forever
With a sweet emotion;
Nothing in the world is single;
All things by a law divine
In one spirit meet and mingle.
Why not I with thine?

See the mountains kiss high heaven
And the waves clasp one another;
No sister-flower would be forgiven
If it disdained its brother;
And the sunlight clasps the earth
And the moonbeams kiss the sea:
What is all this sweet work worth
If thou kiss not me?"

Loves' Philosophy. P.B.Shelley

Shelley's poem, Loves' Philosophy, is the embodiment of connection, and what love in action looks like. Equally, as fear is repulsion in action, it is the antithesis of love. If the rivers feared the oceans, there would be no oceans and without the oceans no rivers. As Shelly says, nothing in the world is single. This guides us to focus now on our absolute and inescapable Element of Connection between all other things.

There can be no doubt that interdependence is a persistent battle for the Ego. That individual Egoism of self interest that motivates and perpetuates our separateness, straining and comparing constantly with others. Negligent of the binding philosophy of the universe, the one song that is love and harmony of all.

At this point, while we are on the subject of Ego, I would suggest noting that the deliberate letting go of Ego is an essential ingredient necessary for the later Element of Intention to work positively for you. In letting go of Ego, a true depth to your connections with the rest of the Universe is enabled, and consequently, an openness to the potentiality within. After all, when it comes down to it, the Universe is the ultimate demonstration of Intention in action.

In understanding, observing, tuning into, and finally cleansing our accepting Connection with all things, we dissolve the Ego that is the source of our suffering.

There are key components in the detail of the last sentence, therefore I'm going to repeat this last sentence once more, but this time, read it slowly and deliberately, with an emphasis on the key important aspects of it.

In UNDERSTANDING, OBSERVING, TUNING INTO and finally CLEANSING our ACCEPTING CONNECTION with all things, we dissolve the Ego, that is the source of our suffering.

I have included several different examples of how the Element of Connection may manifest. Of course, there are an unlimited variety of Connection possibilities, but my first example occurred in the processes of writing this very chapter and came unexpectedly and completely out of the blue, almost as if by design.
Here is what happened. The illustrations my daughter Sophie has drawn are influenced by the book, but are by and large her own creations. While I was interstate, Sophie was spending a weekend of creativity and illustrating, part of which resulted in the creation below. At the time I was not consciously aware of her ideas but did know that she was intending to do some sketching.

The theme Sophie illustrated came about to capture a common, yet not fully understood, type of connection, that of birds in flight together and in particular, birds in murmuration.

Murmuration is the phenomenon in which birds move on mass as if operating as a single entity, often in circumstances of threat or when roosting. Even when numbered in the thousands and flying in close proximity, a connection exists between all the birds which is effortless, silent and unifying. Unknown to myself, at the time of her illustrating, I was over 700 kilometers away and had just experienced an art exhibition comprising 10,000 porcelain starlings, suspended in the act of murmuration. The exhibition demonstrated connection to me in dramatic artistic flair and reinforced to me, my own writing and understanding on the Element of Connection.

Within hours of experiencing this, and without any conscious communication, Sophie had proudly messaged me a photograph of her latest illustration of Connection – that of a flock of birds in murmuration. After gathering myself from the stunned sensation of this incredible and timely message, I replied with a photograph that I had taken at the exhibition to remind myself of Connection in action. In that moment, for Sophie and myself, words did not need to be used, we simply knew together the absolute connection we can experience beyond any traditional comprehension.

Connection is the Element that, if neglected, arguably causes the biggest problems to our wellbeing. It's also the Element that some could describe as the most spiritual. Whilst I don't hold to any single religious persuasion, if there is some form of unifying intelligence, some form of overall consciousness, some form of God or spirit, then I suggest, what flows in Connection, is it.

To make sense of this, in a simplified form, we could say Connection itself is a term describing the relationship between all things. It is the Element that holds everything together; despite our individual perceptions we have as separate identities. As humans, with knowledge, science, discoveries and explorations, we have extended our sensory perceptions of material and non-material connections, but even with this, we don't know what we don't know, that which we don't or can't "see".

When we use the term Connection in our everyday life, we are probably referring to how we relate to and interact with others, in person, using the phone, talking to our friends, listening to our colleagues, looking deeply into the eyes of our loved ones, noticing the body language of those around us or maybe using social media. We may find bigger connections being part of a family, a group, a choir, an orchestra, a sports team, a dance chorus, a motorcycle gang, the community, an army or a nation. The list goes on. But these connections do not even scratch the surface. They are like the tiniest crystal of ice on the tip of the largest iceberg. Connections are everywhere you can see, and everywhere you can't. In fact, it would be more appropriate to say we are all just a part of the whole, it's just the boundary names and our perspective that divides.

Just as we think of ourselves as a single body, one person, one thing, we are at the same time a body comprising trillions of individual cells all connected instantly to one another. Instant messaging apps really are nothing compared to the connection, and with it flow of information, that our individual cells have, which are taking place at the speed of light every nano second, between each of the trillions of cells in your body. Think beyond your own cells too, and see how bacteria helps to nourish, protect and feed your body or live in cooperation with it, and that's just in your body. Then there are the connections in every other body, animal, insect, plant, tree and organism. Each of these collections of connections all in turn connect with each other.

These connections which, to all intents and purposes are a flow of information, are what determines the structure, health and diversity of our self-regulating biosphere, that collection of ecosystems, on which ultimately, our own species depends.

It is more and more challenging in our hectic, multi-media, faced paced, noisy lives to tune into our underlying connections. But that doesn't mean they are not there; it means we are not paying attention to them or being open to them.

Wherever you look you will see Connections if you are open to the nature of them. As I sit here in the early morning light and notice a small round pattern of light reflected onto the inside of the bottom window shutters, I am reminded of Connection. I am at first confused by how a beam of light is cast onto the inside of the closed shutters. Then I see there is a necklace hanging on the dressing table in just the right position to catch sunlight from the top section of the shutters that are slightly open. The glass in the necklace is warmed by the sunlight and is reflecting the light it now has onto the inside of the window shutters, which in turn have a new aspect to them. There is a good example here for Connection; that if we look carefully and openly enough, we can see connecting links between all matter. The sun, necklace, window shutter, my eye, my brain, my fingers writing, and now you have a connecting link and that link has in some way created a new aspect to each component it has connected with.

Most people, when asked to consider examples of deep or unexplained connections, can think of times where events have suggested a Connection beyond the normal physical perspective. One such time occurred with my wife as we sat in our downstairs living room wrapping presents before Christmas in the year 2000. Our third child Freddie had been home from hospital for about a week and was asleep upstairs in a cot in our bedroom. Our elder two daughters were asleep next door in their bedroom. Freddie had been born four weeks premature, but was still of a good average weight for a new born, and was released from hospital after a couple of days. Freddie had no problems since coming home, though of course as a new born premature baby, we were extra cautious with our watch over him. On this particular evening we had decided for the first time to leave Freddie in our bedroom to sleep in his cot, rather than have him downstairs. After about 20 minutes wrapping presents my wife abruptly stopped what she was doing and said "I need to check on Freddie, something isn't right". There were no sounds of crying or movement from the upstairs, but there was no doubt in my wife's heart and mind that something was wrong with Freddie at that precise moment. I considered this a natural and wary response, although there were no indications to me of any concerns. I knew immediately though that we had a problem as my wife got to the cot. Despite being downstairs I heard her desperate words crying out. Words all parents never want to hear "Help? No! He's not breathing.... Freddie.... Help... Robert... No, No."

I leapt up the stairs 4 at a time and was, it seemed, almost instantly in the bedroom. Freddie had stopped breathing. He was limp and had turned blue. My wife passed him eagerly into my arms with absolute dread, panic and frantically questioning what to do. An ambulance was called. Fortunately, with some mouth to mouth, Freddie's breathing returned along with the colour to his cheeks before the ambulance arrived.

Without the connection between Mother and baby, that was inaudibly heard and invisibly seen, Freddie would most likely not be with us today.

As science develops and our understanding of connections and correlations grows, our view of the plethora of intertwinement grows too, right down to the quantum level of entanglement.

To be open ourselves, to both perceiving and understanding these connections, requires us to suspend our reliance on facts based on our ordinary senses, and shift to a state of deep intuition. Each one of us, if we cast our minds back over our lives, and look openly, are sure to find many experiences of connection that may have been dismissed because they seemed beyond physical possibility. There may have been a rational explanation which was just not revealed, but then too, there may have been an explanation beyond our level of consciousness.

One well documented example of this is a series of experiments and subsequent hypothesis created by

Cleve Backster, an ex FBI researcher who specialised in polygraph lie detection. Backster believed he had accidentally hit on this kind of connection on 2nd February 1966. Backster was researching the uptake of water in a dracaena plant. He had hooked up a pair of electrodes to the leaf of the plant to measure what he hypothesised would be a decrease in electrical resistance as the plant absorbed the water. To his surprise, this did not occur, however, eventually there was a change in the contour readings, similar to that of a human exposed to a short duration emotional stimulation and unrelated to the uptake of water. In an attempt to explore this reading, Backster decided to expose the plant to a form of threat to wellbeing as might be done in a human experiment to illicit an emotional response. He decided to subject an adjacent leaf to a dunk into a cup of hot coffee. After nine minutes there was no change in reading. Looking for alternative tests, Backster had a seemingly spontaneous thought; to threaten the leaf which held the electrodes directly, a thought of burning the leaf with a match. At this exact moment, thirteen minutes and fifty-five seconds into the chart reading, there was a dramatic and sustained upsweep in the chart reading. As there was no physical contact between Backster and the plant, it appeared bizarre that in some way, the plant had sensed Backster's thought to burn it's leaf. This experiment was repeated with different instrumentation, different locations, and with the same and different plants. Each yielded similar readings, even when the leaf was removed from the plant.

Backster went on to further test this connective link or perception of fear / threat between two separate organisms. The first of which had been between Backster himself and the plant, then subsequently between the plant and shrimps that were subject to a random drop into boiling water.

Many have disputed Backster's experiments, but when we consider it, the hypothesis of the experiment is no more bizarre than how a person from the 18th century would view the connection of sound and image instantly across space between a transmitter and a television set, or comprehend the invisible connection of entire centuries of information via the tiny devices we use today. For many the problem in being able to believe in its reality stems from the limits of perceptual understanding combined with a non-acceptance without hard core facts.

There are so many unseen connections that it is probably more appropriate to ask, is there anything that ultimately isn't connected? The role of bacteria in our bodies, the synchronised heart beats and brain waves of people who trust one another, the flow of information between trees, the solar wind blowing like a hairdryer across the earth's magnetosphere. Just think of how your own body is physically, continually recycling within the universe. The material composition of each cell being replaced and the old material excreted to eventually take up residence, temporarily, in some other form, creature, plant, ocean, rock.

As the word Connection describes a state between things, let's explore this further. Imagine you meet up with a person you have never met before. Immediately, before you have even spoken, on a sensory level your Connection is taking shape. You have started to familiarise yourself with this person, and they with you. You are sharing information silently of mutual recognition, sight, smell, trustworthiness, respect. Your eyes may meet, you may shake hands. The arrays of conscious and sub-conscious connections are working automatically to determine your type of Connection. As your Connection continues and the depth of it increases, you may begin at some level to adopt aspects of the other, or adapt yourself to the other. You have been changed, enriched or affected to some degree as they have by you. Once you have Connected at this level you will always remain in Connection because the state of each being has been permanently altered. You cannot un-meet or un-connect this flow of information.

If you were to think of the first time you met each of the people in your life, could you identify anyone who you felt uneasy with, and yet you had no solid foundation of fact for that feeling. Alternatively, could you identify anyone who you felt an instant connection with, and likewise no logical explanation as to why? The levels of communication, of connection are indeed vast and at times inexplicable. For the most part they are going on way beyond our level of conscious awareness.

Now consider that you are currently the person you are because of all the people and things you have ever been connected to. Likewise, those people are or were who they are because of all the people they were connected to, including you. So, when you connect with someone, it is not just a connection between two people, but a cascading accumulation of connections. It is a melting pot of the sum of strengths or weaknesses, the kindness or fears, all the multiplicity of interactions within and of all these connections. Not only that, but your current self is entirely unique to that moment because of this fact and can never truly be repeated.

The message here is that on every level, whether it be in our awareness or not, good Connection is a big, big deal. It nurtures our innate needs. Without it we have a void and lack. We become weakened, and in that weakness, we become vulnerable to replacing that lack of good Connection with something that may mask over the missing essential in your life. We may become driven to block out the thoughts and feelings of what is not there or falsely seek to full fill this innate need. A sustained lack of good Connections often then leads to addictive or maladaptive behaviour. Not necessarily drugs or alcohol or gambling or sex, but many other things too like hoarding, eating, exercise, internet and social media addiction, being 'busy' and obsessional thinking. It will also lead to increased feelings of isolation and low self-worth as our own sense of personal value is diminished.

The problem we have with maintaining good connection in the 'advanced world' is not just that we live in more physically isolated families and communities, but that our present competitive human culture presses us to acquire more, go further, faster and greater, buy more, do more and earn more, look slimmer, prettier, be more muscular or unblemished. As this develops, individual identity, separateness and Ego is pushed to grow exponentially to epidemic proportions. But this separation is a disease to our mental and consequently physical wellbeing. Here again, what prevents change is another paradox. As modern humans we seek an ideal of happiness and contentment through a desire to be seen as individually successful. But this is very different from genuine contentment. Success can only be temporary, not only because nothing is permanent, but because once we have it, our Ego tells us we need more. Then the chase continues for further "success". The bigger house, the faster, bigger, more expensive car. We train our children to learn earlier and more, to be top of the class or best in team. If only I had $5,000 spare in the bank, I could be happy, but when that day arrives a new $10,000 goal is needed, and then $20,000, and so on. This doesn't just relate to an individual's Ego, but to that of a group, or a nation. Think of the aimless pursuit of higher GDP (Gross Domestic Product) which is borne primarily from the mass manipulation of the desires and dependencies of individuals to have more, newer, "better" and generally unnecessary things, yet in seeking to full fill this desire, we lose our opportunity for contentment, increase our work time and increase our competitive separateness.

How is this so? Well, in the process of striving, we never arrive for long before we leave again. But also, we alienate or lose our connections with the things that really matter, we forget that we are a part of the whole, and see ourselves only through separateness.

There is an often quoted phrase, of which I am unsure of the original source, but which illustrates well our disconnection from others and into the consumption of what is the Ego. It goes like this "We buy things we don't want, with money we don't have, to impress people we don't like".

What is being conveyed here is the epidemic of disconnecting action that is occurring with the function of making us feel better about ourselves, but in reality, has the effect of increasing the void of positive connections we have. It also leaves us as slaves to consumerism and more deeply trapped in our competitive individuality. Unfortunately, our whole world now is trapped on this conveyer belt of consumerism because the infrastructure, governments and institutions of our society self perpetuate and expedite disconnection. It's ironic, and a perfect illustration of paradox that as our mobile telecommunications technology advances from analog to digital, 2G to 3G, to 4G and 5G and so forth, with the objective of increasing connection, that the greater the advances, the more this serves as a disconnection, as a tool which is unconsciously used to feed the needs of the Ego, reduce our genuine connections, and at the same time be the behaviour we go to to subjugate our loneliness.

Phone, phone in my hand, who is the fairest in the land!

Social media, networking and addiction to image are what we might call "illusions of Connection". They are one of the real obstacles to good Connection in our current times. Social media and networking offer us a fantastic tool for Connection. We can now connect to anyone, anywhere, at any time. But there is also a greater opportunity for false image, a greater manipulation of user information and a more distorted image that is more often than not a tool for the Ego, a counter-connection. Particularly amongst the young, this virtual world of connections is infiltrating the real world. Through creating a distorted image and false Connection in the virtual world, we can become sensitive to being caught out as less than our virtual self when seen in the real world. This can lead to spending more and more time preparing our own image, and getting caught up in masking the "real" self.

Truly positive, effective Connection must be genuine, non-judgemental and with a purity of Attention.

Remember, Ego is a barrier to good Connection. It's a barrier because the Ego sees itself as being separate and more important. It doesn't see the equality and interconnectedness of life, matter, everything. The Ego will feel judged, and will judge, and so will negate any available quality in Connection.

The German philosopher Arthur Schopenhauer expressed our connections with other living creatures when he wrote:

"Individuation is but an appearance in a field of space and time, these being the conditioning forms through which my cognitive faculties apprehend their objects. Hence the multiplicity and differences that distinguish individuals are likewise but appearances. They exist, that is to say, only in mental representation. My own true inner Being actually exists in every living creature, as truly and immediately known as my own consciousness in myself."

Begin now with these specific ways in which you can maximise Connection with your environment or with another person:

1. Eliminate distraction. Deliberately decide to use all your focus as practiced with the Element of Attention.

2. Sit quietly with another person who is happy to practice this too. Hold each other's hands just for 1 minute in silence, focusing just on the sensation of the other hands touching yours. Next for one minute, look into their eyes, and in turn describe

the colours you see in the iris. Finally, aim to spend a few minutes with your Connection partner to tune your individual senses together. This may be in a garden, beach or place of beauty. Work through each of your senses in turn describing carefully and in detail what you see, hear, feel, smell. The sayings heart to heart, holding hands, speaking with one voice, seeing eye to eye are descriptions of great Connection because they are exclusively devoted to experiencing with the same view, emotion, feeling or voice.

3. Allow time with your connections, stay with them, and resist the pull away from them which maybe a sense of awkwardness, fear, hate, boredom or false urgency to move on.

4. When your connections are disrupted by self-centred urges. Be silent and still as your Ego feels the need to push its point and profess its righteousness, cleverness or languish in adulation. Witness then how the silence you have kept allows your presence in the Connection to your inner, peaceful self grow.

5. Next, as all things are connected and held together by energy, frequency and vibration, try this practice now with your Connection to the vibration of music with Elgar's uplifting masterpiece, "Nimrod" to illustrate the flow of Connection:

Find a comfortable space. If you are inside, close your eyes as you begin to listen to the music. If you are lucky enough to be outside on a quiet sunny day, raise your eyes to the sky, as you tune in to the crescendo sounds of "Nimrod".

Now, put your attention into your own internal space and visualise the sounds as they travel through those spaces as well as the material of each cell and atom within your body, resonating, reverberating and for the moments they travel through, influencing and holding each in the musical vibrations captivating grasp. Allow each tiny part of your body to be overcome and controlled by the sounds you hear. When the music is done... stay silent for a few minutes staying with the lingering feelings that have run through and connected with you.

There is no need to wonder why it is that music can raise the fine hairs of the body, shatter glass, and create tears in the eyes... it is in reality a Connection with the flow of spirit which moves through the soul. Next time you do this, find one of your favourite pieces of music, close your eyes, and deeply listen in the same way. Do you feel the draw into the beat, the guidance of the frequency, and vibration of the sounds in the melody? Connect to it. Sing out loud or in your head. Let your body sway to the beat or stir your soul. Allow the hairs to rise on the back of your neck and your stomach to sense its own void. Everything has a vibration, and music is a pure and deliberate human version of it. As Nikola Tesla one of the greatest scientific minds in recorded history said;

"If you want to find the secrets of the universe,

think in terms of energy, frequency, and vibration."

Take a moment now to visualise yourself, the essence of you, as separate from your body. See yourself from this vantage point without physical identity. What you are without the skin and bone, the labels and statuses that are seen by yourself and others in the physical world. Now look at others and see them in the same way. Here, seeing beyond the Ego we are all connected, we are all one.

Get connecting.

Go forward now and use both your Attention and Reflection to strengthen the quality of your connections, and the internal Elements that come in the following chapter. Observe how your own quiet magnificence elevates your contentment in its peaceful relationship with the world, and so too the peacefulness of the world itself.

Finally. Take a moment to consider some Reflections and then write these down:

1. What is one key realisation or reinforcement of your own experience of Connection that you can take away from this chapter?
2. What could you improve on in your use of the Element of Connection?
3. What have you done well in your use of the Element of Connection?

**Chapter Five
The Spokes**

Element Five : Attraction

*"Mind is the Master power that mould and makes,
And Man is Mind, and evermore he takes
The tool of thought, and, shaping what he wills,
Brings forth a thousand joys, a thousand ills:-
He thinks in secret, and it comes to pass:
Environment is but his looking glass."*

As a man thinketh. James Allen.

As with all the Elements in Being, the Element of Attraction in our lives is non-material, non-physical, meta-physical. It is also interdependent on the other Elements and dictates how the material and physical dimensions, as well as the pathways in our life, are brought about.

The quality of positivity in the pathways of life that

you attract or manifest, whether they be relationships, opportunities, wellbeing or peacefulness, depend on the genuine nature and composition of your other Elements in Being as they interface with your Element of Attraction.

When I talk about Attraction, I'm not talking specifically here about the way you felt that indescribable pull towards the love of your life when they first caught your eye over a crowded room, though perhaps there is something in that too. The attraction I am talking about has much broader implications to your life, a bit like a behind the scenes guidance system or kind of homing device, sometimes referred to as the "law of attraction".

In a really basic sense, we attract what we think, feel and subsequently do. Or, more succinctly we could say, we attract what we are.

In the words of Bruce Lee and Buddha:

"The mind is everything, what you think you become."

And the from the bible Proverbs 23:7:

"As a man thinketh in his heart, so is he."

Of course, it isn't quite as simplistic as that. If all we had to do was think long and hard enough about our desires in order to attract them into our lives, then we would all be rich, content and happy, and I and countless others could give up our work.

Though it is not a simple single act to deliberately manifest, this phenomenon is an observable occurrence in our everyday lives, ever acting on and constantly drawing out our material realities. Whether the Attraction is one of kindness, fear, peace, blame, success or failure. That which is prominent firstly in our hearts, and secondly in our thoughts, we attract.

Additionally, those we have Connection to in our lives attract what we each become. You know that being around a peaceful person has a calming effect on all those nearby. When faced with an irritated and angry encounter, it is not easy to remain calm. Happiness too is contagious. Research has shown that spending time with a happy friend increases happiness, and that this happiness extends beyond, by degrees of separation, to those you haven't even met. That is because they have increased others happiness, and in turn those you may encounter. Consequently, they have increased your happiness and you theirs, in the same way that a disease spreads.

Even on a cellular level, it is now being discovered that once individual cells in our body become old, their communication with other younger cells nearby will be to influence them that they should be old, and this then "infects" their age negatively.

At age 17, unknowing the deeper meaning behind what l was about to do, l did something that was ultimately to teach me a valuable lesson. A lesson that l have only in the last few years come to reflect on and truly understand.

I was walking home late at night after visiting my new girlfriend. From a dark side street, her previous boyfriend, recently jilted, had been covertly waiting to confront me. As I approached the side street he jumped out and began to abuse me, provoking me to fight him. I explained that I had no desire to fight with him. I've never been a fighter, in a physical sense, and the idea even when being deliberately provoked, just didn't sit right with me. The fella threw a punch which missed. Next, in what may have seemed like a dangerous move, I spontaneously decided to lay on the ground. I thought, then calmly told him my thoughts, I'm not going to, and I have no wish to fight you, I have no argument with you.

It was indeed a reckless moment, but then again, I was a teenager with an unrealistic, invincible view of myself. The fella in question was dumbstruck, but most importantly he had attracted a calmness from me which had deflated his anger. Not knowing quite what to do, he slowly and quietly walked away, shaking his head in disbelief. It was almost as if he had his tail between his legs. I don't of course know what he was thinking, but I do know what the affect was on him.

When we choose what to receive or refuse from others, we remain independent in our emotions, and lose any need to exert control over them. The result is, we attract what is beneficial to us, rather than attempting to fight against what is not.

The ancient story below illustrates further this law of Attraction and how with supreme discipline, practice and letting go of Ego, the pull of negative Attraction can be altered to the positive.

It goes something like this:

There once lived a great warrior. Though quite old, he still could defeat any challenger. His reputation extended far and wide throughout the land, and many students gathered to study under him.

One day an infamous young warrior arrived at the village. He was determined to be the first man to defeat the great master. Along with his strength, he had an uncanny ability to spot and exploit any weakness in an opponent. He would wait for his opponent to make the first move, thus revealing a weakness, and then would strike with merciless force and lightning speed. No one had ever lasted with him in a match beyond the first move.

Much against the advice of his concerned students, the old master gladly accepted the young warrior's challenge. As the two squared off for battle, the young warrior began to hurl insults at the old master. He threw dirt and spit in his face. For hours, he verbally assaulted him with every curse and insult known to mankind. But the old warrior merely stood there motionless and calm. Finally, the young warrior exhausted himself. Knowing he was defeated, he left feeling shamed.

Somewhat disappointed that he did not fight the

insolent youth, the students gathered around the old master and questioned him. "How could you endure such an indignity? How did you drive him away?"

"If someone comes to give you a gift and you do not receive it," the master replied, "to whom does the gift belong?"

Reflecting on this story we can see that there was still a fight occurring between the youth and the warrior. This wasn't a physical fight however, but one of calmness over aggression, one side would have to succumb to the other eventually. Don't we all have control of what we wish to receive (or attract)? If we are aware of our thoughts and feelings, and are resolute in our quiet rejection of the "gift", we not only determine what we attract, but become a brave warrior. In this situation, who and what was the greatest strength and what did it attract?

The calmness and rejection of aggression from the master, within his heart and his thoughts, ultimately attracted the same from the challenging youth.

There are countless varieties and examples of the Element of Attraction at play. Another example of this phenomenon in action, yet on an entirely different level, is that of water-divining. This peculiar method used to locate hidden water is somewhat of a mystery. The practice involves the diviner holding one end of a right-angled thin metal rod or wire loosely in each hand with the other angle pointing forwards. The diviner then slowly moves forward simply focusing his thoughts intently on water. If the rods or wires move and cross, then it is indicated that this is the point water can be found. The practice is so successful that it is not uncommon for utility companies to have, in their employ, water diviners. In addition, it seems divining is not restricted to water with some people. If the diviner's thoughts are on something else, then the same results will apply. How can we make sense of this? I will leave you to draw your own conclusions, but I will say this. It is clear that when we tune in to our thoughts and feelings. When we consistently know in our hearts, and consciously focus without doubt on what we believe them to be, then this is what turns up for us. This is what we attract.

Remember;
What you consistently think, feel in your heart, and subsequently do, is what you attract.

As always, there is a word of warning. There is a component of this principle that is often missed which sabotages positive attraction.

The law of attraction states that we attract what we are focused on. If we have a mind that is repeatedly dwelling on something that we desperately desire in our life, this want becomes a central one in our lives. But behind this desire is an opposite and founding driver that usurps the attraction of our desires. That opposite is a lack, which if prominent, will actually lead to being the attraction in our life, that is to say; we display a greater level of thoughts, feelings and behaviours that attract more lack.

Let us say for example that you are unhappy with your current job. Your motivation wanes, your sleep is affected, and your focus becomes heavily weighted on leaving. Your thinking becomes focused on what you don't have, what is missing. This is when your thoughts increase the missing components in your work, when paradoxically you need to be without this resistance, and have an acceptance of what is, in order to allow a focus on what you desire.

You may spend many hours trawling through the Internet and newspapers searching for a new position. If this searching comes from a place of discontent for what is, then that is the driving force for your Attraction. You are searching not so much because of what you have, but because of what you don't have (what you lack).

Thus, unless we are lucky (and sometimes we may be), we simply attract more of what we don't have, that is, we stay the same. This becomes a circle of discontent because our awareness and thoughts are trapped in a focus on how the things that we desire are beyond our reach, and that the odds are stacked against us. The more we focus on the odds stacked against us, the more they are stacked against us!

By the same principle, if we are content with where we are, if we can accept and even have Gratitude for what is, even if that is difficult, then we no longer become focused on what we lack.

It is also vital to point to the essential ingredient with which we must live our lives, if our attractions are to be positive and we are to remove ourselves more completely from the 'I want' problem. This ingredient is altruism, via empathy and non-judgement. These aspects of ourselves are the cornerstones of the peaceful preservation of ourselves, our society, community, diversity of species and our planet, which comes about through our unconditional desire to improve the wellbeing of others and the environment.

We will return again later in the book to work on maintaining the practical changes for all our Elements in Being. For this moment and for the Element of Attraction we will look at the words I AM instead of I WANT.

What we say after the words I AM, gradually dictates what we attract and magnify in our life, and what we say after the words I WANT has a counter-effect to what we would like to attract.

As you become an experienced practitioner of these principles, you will realise that I AM on its own is very powerful, and ultimately all you need. It is an accepting statement of both what is and a faith in yourself, that what you need for any situation is inherently within you. For our current purposes however, we can add some key pointers to follow the words I AM.

Begin now to practice your Element of Attraction, while you are surging forward towards mastery of your Elements in Being.

Here are the key words to follow I AM with in order to magnify the good stuff today:

* I am an appreciator of beauty -
Beauty and gratitude appear in my life.

* I am on purpose -
I am less distracted and naturally move towards my goals.

* I am a resistor of enculturation -
I value my own unique self and become more genuine.

* I am welcome to the unknown -
The undiscovered manifests, new opportunity arises.

* I am highly enthusiastic -
Passion, devotion and joy appear.

* I am inner in my direction -
I am less reactive and move towards my own essential self.

* I am detached from outcome -
I accept whatever happens and become more present.

* I am independent of the good opinion of others –
Another's view is based only on their experienced perspective and could only be that way, as is mine.

* I am without the need to exert control over others -
I have no anguish because of how others are, nor will controlling others allow the magnificent me to be seen.

* I am connected with all living creatures as truly and immediately as I am with myself.

Amazingly, when these are practiced, there is a natural elimination of the phrase beginning I WANT.

The gifts these "I am" statements bring are beyond any other, for as they remove "I want", they consequently remove lack from your life, and open the barrier you had self-imposed that prevented positive attraction.

Finally. Take a moment to consider some Reflections and then write these down:

1. What is one key realisation or reinforcement of your own knowledge of the Element of Attraction that you can take away?
2. What could you improve on in your use of the Element of Attraction?
3. What have you done well in your use of the Element of Attraction?

Element Six : Meaning

"He who has a why to live can bear almost any how"

Friedrich Nietzsche

Victor Frankl, was an Austrian Psychiatrist who found his own extraordinary meaning in the survival and documentation of his experiences of life in the Nazi concentration camps. In his book "Man's search for meaning", he described these experiences, and then based the foundation of his whole brand of existential therapy, Logotherapy, on meaning. In referring to Frankl and tying in my own view of meaning and it's role in our wellbeing and survival, I hope to illustrate how even the sometimes torturous process of finding meaning in all that occurs in our life, whether that be the disturbing, disastrous or excruciatingly painful, is ultimately an action which elevates our resistant being and takes it to a place it didn't yet want to go, but once there is wise beyond measure.

The Element of Meaning as a starting point relates particularly to the situational circumstances of a person's life. These individual situations build the broader Meaning of our life, and ultimately our destiny, both individually and as a society. In the context of this book, it is appropriate to put our focus on finding the Meaning in the situational to allow us to find our own broader Meaning. Finding this Meaning is akin to looking at life through a new lens and creates a perspective that leads to positive change, despite what may often be the most torturous of circumstances.

With all mental suffering comes a resistance to what is seen to cause the suffering. This is perfectly logical of course. However, without this resistance the mental suffering itself would cease. That is not to say that pain will cease, or that the emotions that accompany life events will numb. But finding your Meaning within any given situation is fundamental in being able to stop your resistance to what is current in your life and thereby release the suffering. The difficulty is that to find Meaning in many challenging situations can seem impossible. Even being able to consider Meaning when a person is in a state of grief, loss, fear, hopelessness or other mood affected state is particularly difficult and further adds to its elusiveness.

Meaning then, is principally about the thoughts and feelings surrounding the final purpose, reason or significance of an outcome, the why of what is. If a valid or beneficial why can be found when previously none was apparent, then a useful Meaning has become available which will in some way release resistance and with it, mental suffering. In turn, having found the why, an opening to how a situation can be endured or navigated becomes available, and along with it the motivation to carry this through.

To further complicate the understanding of the end purposes of a situation or event, especially ones that are causing suffering, the Meaning might also be entirely non-obvious. What possible purpose could there be in losing a loved one before they had fully lived their life, or to have to endure the abuse of a violent 'carer' as a child? As sentient beings we look for Meaning, yet often times Meaning is inconceivable. The ability to make sense of the world is a source of great power and allows us to advance beyond all other creatures in the control of our environment, but sometimes we cannot find a sense or Meaning that is either positive or good to us. This is the point at which our mental suffering grows, and it seems is also the point at which our path towards religious or spiritual beliefs will either form or fail. We may fill the void in the understanding of Meaning with a religious or spiritual explanation, or dismiss religion as being incongruous with our suffering, with thoughts such as; how could any loving God allow this suffering?

To illustrate the type of torturous search that

occasionally has to occur in the search for meaning, Ram Dass, the American spiritual teacher, former academic and clinical psychologist wrote a letter some years ago to parents who had tragically lost their daughter in a senseless, violent murder. The letter is in itself a search for meaning which, like our own searches for meaning, requires us to at times elevate ourselves from the oppressive all-consuming pits of despair and suffering,to a narrow ledge high on a vertical cliff from where a perspective of vulnerable, terrifying heights causes our legs to tremble and our head to spin, but at the same time allows meaning to be found.

In his letter, Ram Dass begins with is an open, clear, unobstructed acknowledgement of the pain and thus a validation of it. He then takes this acknowledgement further, calling out the agony with compassion and love, as something that cannot and should not be soothed by anyone, because deep within, Meaning must be found.

It is a brutally pure example of one of the most frightening nightmares a human could imagine experiencing, that of the violent death of one's child, and teaches us the absolutely central role that Meaning has in creating a pathway to somehow navigate a narrow dark and winding route through our suffering.

There are of course as many meanings as there are circumstances. Our individual meanings like every Element will have its own unique aspects for our Being, but the wholesomeness and deeper benefit that a particular Meaning may provide our wellbeing will depend on the dominance of our Ego. Beyond a well-balanced life, with a stable home, healthy relationships with others, fresh unprocessed food, and appropriate exercise, contributing something of ourself to a positive cause for others is a Meaning which nourishes wellbeing and enriches our life. In environments where Ego flourishes, Meaning is focused not on others but on the self. In this respect the value of Meaning is lost as it masquerades as a force for wellbeing, but in doing so, becomes a virus to Connection.

What Meaning does a worker bee have? Ultimately, it is to collect nectar to turn into honey to feed the hive and as a byproduct to pollinate the flowers. Its Meaning is an act for the benefit of others, and is done so in Connection with all the other bees in the hive, with the flowers and the vibration of the flowers' fragrances. Now imagine if bees lost the Meaning of this act. Imagine instead they all had an individual sense of their own importance, and spent their days languishing in the hive. What would happen to their wellbeing? Within a very short space of time, the plants would fail, the bees would lose their food and they would die. Fortunately for us all and for the bees, their Meaning is inherent. But often for our complex human species Meaning is more illusive. It may sound like a far-removed analogy, but if correct alignment with meaning is so crucial for a bee, then wouldn't it be equally important to a human?

If we search openly for our meanings, then not only will greater value be brought into life, but also too the strength to find a 'how' to navigate whatever life throws our way.

Start today to consider what meanings you have discovered through your experience of suffering.

In what ways have you grown because of your own unique suffering?

Whatever your circumstances, you are here, right now where you are supposed to be. The place you are in may feel like rock bottom, or it may seem as though it is moving more positively. Either way, navigating it will happen somehow. That how will be determined by the level of value you find in its meaning.

1. Take ten minutes to be as comfortable as you can in peaceful attention to this present moment.
2. Observe yourself and your own presence as if you are looking at your own self from outside
3. Notice that you are not your body, you are beyond this.
4. Notice that what you observe, including yourself depends upon, influences and creates the flow of each aspect of the moment.
5. Everything is ultimately circulating, moving eventually to a return of form and at its own pace, influenced by everything else, but it's Meaning is to be found here and now in order to create the next here and now.
6. Your Meaning is to value what is, so that you can

value what isn't. If you are in pain, the Meaning is to allow you to value non-pain. If you are grieving, it is to value the lost. If you are sad, it is to value joy. Without, allows us to value with.

Ultimately then, having found the Meaning allows us to give away something of ourselves. As we become wise through our meanings, we can impart wisdom to others.

Finally. Take a moment to consider some Reflections and then write these down:

1. What is one key realisation or reinforcement of your own knowledge of Meaning that you can take away?
2. What could you improve on in your use of the Element of Meaning?
3. When have you used your Element of Meaning well?

Chapter Seven: Intention

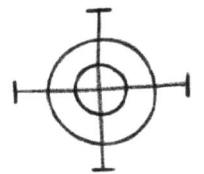

"Everything is energy. Match the frequency of the reality you want and you cannot help but get that reality. It can be no other way. This is not philosophy. This is physics."

Albert Einstein.

Einstein uses the word "want" in the quote above, but as we know, wants can cause us difficulties. A purer, clearer and more positive word we can use, which is the essence of what Einstein is pointing at, is intention. I say this because of the paradoxical nature of the thoughts and feelings associated with "I want" that point more often than not to the underlying lack, as discussed previously in the Element of Attraction. My choice and use of the word Intention though is without lack, and therefore, if used to replace want, becomes all-powerful.

So, what does Einstein mean when he says "match the frequency of the reality you want"? Part of the answer may lie with Nikola Tesla, which is ironic considering the less than complimentary regard Einstein had for Tesla. When Einstein had been asked what it was like to be the smartest man alive, he seemingly sarcastically declared that he didn't know and that they had better ask Tesla! Tesla was clearly a genius though and, despite the dubiousness of their mutual respect, had a view that seems to support Einstein's quote above.

As mentioned before in the Element of Connection, Tesla advised;

"If you want to find the secrets of the universe, think in terms of energy, frequency and vibration."

To return to our opening quote on the Element of Intention, if we are to assume that Einstein and Tesla are right, then energy and frequency are central to the secrets of the universe, and along with vibration are a creator. But do we as humans unwittingly use frequency to create the realities of our life both beneficial (our clear intentions) and detrimental (the fixation we have on our lack)?

Our thoughts, conscious and subconscious, are extremely powerful and deliver signalled information, or what might be better described as frequencies, throughout our body and beyond. These signals ultimately form and change both our biological, physical, material and psychological realities.

Studies and research on Telomeres, the 'flogglebinder' on the end of our DNA which acts as a protector to the DNA, show compelling signs that stress is one of the key factors in the wearing away of the Telomeres, and additionally, a calm contented existence over time can extend the Telomeres length. The health of our internal environment is determined not just by what we put into our bodies, but by the power within our internal signalling. If you doubt this, you only need to look at the difference in physical health between the grieving Mother or the stressed, bullied self-doubting worker, and the couple deeply in love or the valued, confident and respected child, parent, friend, neighbour or employee. Over time, anyone in these positions will see considerable effect, either positive or negative, on their physical health, each atom in the body connected, formed and informed by frequency, the vibration and energy.

Therefore, the most important factor to take into account is the difference we can create in our lives with a deliberate use of intention, as opposed to "I want". By using the Element of Intention, what we are doing is describing turning one's attention to, or stretching out toward, some form of desired attainment regardless of a lack. The lack in this case is of no concern; it is not the driver of our action or thinking or even of our feelings. With clear intention there is a sense that getting to an outcome will occur regardless of anything else, no matter how slim the chance or realistic the possibility. In its own time, in the end, the intention will find its way of coming into being.

Each one of us, if we search our memories may find many occasions when we had wanted something really badly, yet the more we tried to get to the want the more elusive it became, yet upon letting go, not of the underlying intention, but of the lack, we found that the elusive thing came to be. Like the common occurrence of many couples who are desperately trying for a baby and cannot fall pregnant only to find, after they resign themselves to not ever being able to have a child, that they are pregnant. They have let go of the lack and their intention has found its way to fulfilment.

Exploring deeper what comprises this meaning of Intention, we see that it involves something of the future and of the present. Here in the present we are visualising, imagining or thinking, with belief about a state, as if we were already living it in the future. This will make available the almost subliminal attention to opportunities that now avail themselves to you in the present, that without having intention, you would normally be blind to.

This state of being is moving beyond the ordinary and into the extraordinary state of inspiration, inspired, in spirit.

I suggest that the specific frequency of Intention is not simply confined to human thinking; it is more specifically a force that we may harness and that manifests for us. When we regard intention as it occurs through the human form, we can see that our whole self; thoughts, feelings and behaviours, our gut and our heart, are not only a force within the universe, but a force from which anything is possible.

Now take that thought and imagine that at a normal level, the movement towards any Intention is 0% and flat, your beliefs are ambivalent and there is no real advancement. Next, consider that being in an unhindered clear belief state of intention, is 100% above your normal operating level. Here you are 100% directed towards your intention. Now, when you introduce a want that is focused on the lack in your life, where you have a deep-seated frustration and annoyance to the lack, or a missing, here your underlying beliefs are not in line with your intention. Conversely, in this situation, you are 100% directed away from your intention. The difference between the two opposites is 200%. In this situation your intention is so hindered by the focus on lack that you would be better off having no intention at all, rather than having two opposites pulling at each other in some bizarre and unseen tug of war.

Let's take a moment to consider the importance of intention and how it grows from general thinking. If you take a look around you, you will see the manifestation of human intention everywhere. From the concrete in the pavement you walk on, to the fillings in your teeth, From the fertiliser on the plants to the tiniest screw in the hinge of your glasses, each exists because of intention. Even if you are in some remote corner or outpost of the planet, you are unlikely to be naked and without some modified environment. You will have some form of shelter; some implements to assist you. These are all physical manifestations of multiple intentions.

Intentions are not just restricted to the physical. In this respect intention becomes a most powerful Element for our work here. When we look at each of the Elements In Being discussed, Intention can bring these Elements further into our being with greater understanding, belief and focus. Each of our Elements exponentially feed and grow one another.

Intention achieves activation after our general thinking becomes applied, and focused to a specific purpose or in a targeted direction, and then moves beyond our conscious awareness. If Intention remains dominant in our conscious, it doesn't always create a positive effect. Here, Intention can be sabotaged by our expectations, and we can enter a dangerous pathway. We may become attached to an outcome that may sound innocuous, but is actually a trap. The trap is the hold that the outcome has over our thinking, this has been recognised over the centuries by many people.

Again, Tilopa said, "Have a mind that is open to everything, but attached to nothing". The outcomes we are focused on and that we hold our attachment to, will then often adjust our Attention, away from the present. This then leaves a serious void in our being, disrupting our Element of Connection, creating a sense of disconnect with ourselves and with the only moment we can participate in. In this state of attachment to the future, we are constantly striving and never arriving, because even if we achieve our expected outcome, we will then experience a short sense of elation, followed by an emptiness as we have lost the work and effort that is part of that attachment.

To escape this emptiness our mind will then automatically move to the next expectation or outcome, and so the cycle of lack, unfulfillment and discontent is perpetuated. Additionally, if we are sufficiently without belief in our intention and are railing against the "what is" of our life, then getting to our intention will be a never ending and thankless task.

To sum up the key points of this Element:
Intention starts as a conscious, clear belief and visualisation of the feelings you will experience as you reach your intention, as if they are already happening, that there is no doubt about this in your heart and mind. It is without attachment to the outcome. That is although you truly know this Intention is your destiny, you accept that it is entirely ok if it does not manifest 'on your Ego's time' or quite as you expect. What you want must be given over to your Intention to remove the draw into a focus on lack.

Here, as in so many ways, we can see the complex interaction and effects which occur between the Elements In Being both in positive and negative ways. As you become attuned to each Element, you will see this more and more.

Start this today:

Take a few minutes before you go to bed to think about what you would like to be doing in one, or two years' time. Take out a pen and paper and write down what that is.

Be as specific as you can. Describe in detail what you will be doing, what you will be thinking about and feeling in this new attained situation.

Reading back through your descriptions several times will start to commit these to your subconscious.

Repeat the reading of your Intention each night visualising yourself experiencing it fully.

Continue to add and embellish the written detail you are describing.

Do not go beyond 10 minutes with this and be sure afterwards to move your thinking back to the present moment, with an activity that uses your Element of Attention in the present moment, such as scanning your body sensations progressively in your mind or focusing on each breath as it leaves and enters your body.

Finally. Take a moment to consider some Reflections and then write these down:

1. What is one key realisation or reinforcement of your own knowledge of Intention that you can take

away?
2. What could you improve on in your use of the Element of Intention?
3. What have you done well in your use of the Element of Intention?

Element Eight : Gratitude

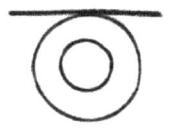

"Gratitude is riches and complaint is poverty."

Doris Day

As we continue this journey, weaving our own understanding of each Element In Being, look also to the thread that runs between each chapter. The dependence of each Element on the other Element as they stitch and knot to form the fabric of your life.

Now, we have Gratitude. Here in this one simple noun, no matter what our financial, physical or mental position, we have the opportunity to connect with life's intrinsic riches. Gratitude is the antithesis of complaint, and complaining is our reinforcing reaction to what we haven't got. In Doris Day's description this equates to our poverty, or perhaps less drastically, it is our wants. Have you noticed how that insatiable four-letter word keeps rearing its head to sabotage our contentment and divert our focus to the missing in our life rather than the present?

We can see that the Element of Gratitude is not some wishy-washy act of nicety, but an instant hit of wellbeing. Gratitude for things in one's life is a simple way of improving contentment. If we are openly, honestly and naturally grateful for what is in our life, then we are living with more than just acceptance, more than appreciation or thankfulness. We are living with a deeply rooted knowing and recognition of the true value of what we experience, as we experience it.

The display of gratitude is a natural acknowledgment of these experiences in our life. To be able to do this absolutely and completely, we need to reflect upon, have attention of, make a connection to, and know the meaning of our life experiences. The Element of Gratitude itself requires these other Elements; Reflection, Attention, Connection and Meaning to be truly beneficial.

The benefits of being grateful extend beyond ourselves too. They include those people who may also come to define who we are. Being able to honour someone else's gift of presence, as an experience in our own life, is a gift in itself and nurtures the recipient as much as the giver. Beyond these immediate benefits of gratitude there lies a deeper but subtly positive effect on our thinking style.

As discussed previously, there is a general and natural tendency to think about what we haven't got in our lives. If this thinking is restrained, logical and deliberate then it is a useful process. However, so often this is not the case. Thinking then becomes far from helpful. Whether it is thinking about what or who we have lost, missed out on or don't seem to be able to get, it is a debilitating thinking state if it is not kept in check.

Understandably, there are situations in life that occur which create this thinking pattern. A form of regret, rumination, resistance or dissatisfaction with our lot in life, leads to an antagonistic relationship with our current status and because of this, we forget about or don't truly value or acknowledge, with gratitude, the wonderful parts of our present life that are right in front of our noses. Managing this can become very difficult, even in the "normal" hectic lives we lead, but especially in those times of grief or loss, anxiety, hopelessness and depression, where thinking itself, is already under incredible strain.

Starting today, make the change from complaint to gratitude:

At lunch time, make a note on paper of all the things you have been unhappy, offended or complained about since you got up this morning, even if they are just thoughts and you haven't verbally expressed them at the time.

In the afternoon, seek out the good, the beautiful,

the useful and helpful. If you are unsure as to whether or not something is appropriate for this definition, ask yourself whether you would miss not having this in your life if it were impossible to have it again. Write down anything that you are glad of that makes you feel gratitude, and that without which your afternoon would be poorer.

In the evening look down each list, the morning list and the afternoon list. Ask yourself do any of the morning complaints really matter now? And, will they matter to me this time tomorrow, next week, next year?

Now ask yourself; has complaining changed the situation for the better and improved my well being?

Next, look at the afternoon list of gratitudes and ask yourself, what do I normally miss appreciating that I would be sad to lose for ever?

Additionally, over the next week, agree with a couple of friends or family members to take the time each day to declare to each other two things for which are grateful. These can be as simple as the clean water that comes through your tap. To the house you live in, to the smile you received from the shop assistant. Go into your gratitude more deeply to uncover the meaning that this particular gratitude brings to each person. For example, the water sustains life, allows you to wash your body, your clothes, your home, it waters your garden and cleans your windows, it cools your face on a hot day and becomes the ice in your drinks.

To reach contentment we must look with gratitude, and in the right places, for those things that nourish our hearts, not adorn our heads like trinkets or jewels.

As Shakespeare describes;

*"My Crown is in my heart, not on my head:
Not deck'd with Diamonds, and Indian stones:
Nor to be seen: my Crown is call'd Content,
A Crown it is, that seldom Kings enjoy."*

King Henry VI, Part 3

Before moving to your final Reflections, contemplate how other Elements work together with Gratitude and the role that "want" plays in negatively focusing each of these Elements and along with it your level of contentment.

Finally. Take a moment to consider some Reflections and then write these down:

1. What is one key realisation or reinforcement of your own knowledge of Gratitude that you can take away?
2. What could you improve on in your use of the Element of Gratitude?
3. How has your past use of the Element of Gratitude benefited your wellbeing?

Element Nine : Loving kindness

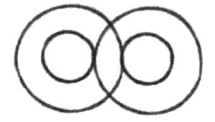

"Where the heart is full of kindness, which seeks no injury to another, either in act or in thought or wish, this full love, creates an atmosphere of harmony, whose benign power touches with healing all who come within its influence. Peace in the heart radiates peace to other hearts, even more surely than contention breeds contention."

Patanjali

The active, genuine display of our Loving Kindness is the most precious gift we can give away. It is impossible to extol highly enough the virtue which is loving kindness, though of course it does not flow freely to all things from all humans. What a world that would look like?

There are clearly degrees to which each one of us is able to extend our Loving Kindness or not, as the case may be. But the fact is, that if we are operating on a highly conscious level, then we have the ability to override automatic emotional responses, and challenge otherwise hidden, encultured or biased thinking, and consequently change how to be with others.

Often though, choosing to be benevolent requires us to move several degrees further and become altruistic. To put others before ourselves. Once more, there is a paradox here because the act of putting others first has such a positive effect on ourselves, that in essence, we are actually being kind to ourselves beyond the measure of any act devoted solely to ourself, or putting ourselves first. We must therefore let go of our ego, to suspend our own little self that says I am more important, I have to be the one who is best, or right, or first, even on some occasions to put ourselves in potential danger. If we can suspend this part of us that is so consumed with the narrow focus of our own self-interest that it finds it difficult to wear the shoes of the other, and that is not able to stop and empathise. If we then simply kick of our shoes and wear theirs. If we can empathise, listen and seek out their view of the world without judgement, then we display a kindness of greater magnitude than could in any other way be possible. In this there is a valuing of a person which is based on love rather than fear, superiority or priority.

There are many circumstances when achieving this may seem impossible, perhaps even immoral. Completely counter to your own beliefs and life experience. To make this goal of sending out Loving

Kindness happen, to choose empathy, means we have to be quite deliberate in keeping a separateness, or non-attachment, from our own moral compass. In the sending of Loving kindness, we are not assuming the position of another, but acknowledging that this is purely their view of the world and is the only perspective that they have available to them in that moment, in the same way our perspective of the world is for ourselves.

When it is hard to send Loving Kindness to another because of their own fears and behaviours, a way of helping to activate this Element is to visualise that there is a line separating you and the other person. Imagine then, that this line is a barrier to taking on or responding resistantly to the other person's fears. Instead you simply hear, see and even empathise with whatever is on the other side of the line in the other person. But you will not be 'infected' by or hold the upset, annoyance or fear that comes with it because of the other's emotion. If you were to step over the line and try to counter their position, profess or argue for what you consider is right, you would become 'infected' with their emotion. But though you can't step over the line, you can send Loving kindness across. No matter what you hear from the other person across the line, Loving kindness is all that you will be able to send back the other way.

In a world of dichotomy, fear is the polar opposite of Loving kindness. As we know from the Element of Attraction, what we think about and feel in our hearts we attract, so if we are in fear and interact with another person, then a fear response will be what we get back, unless we are interacting with a highly conscious, self-actualised individual. It is in these very moments that, if we are to armour ourselves against the attraction of fear, we must defend ourselves and the unwitting deliverer of fear with loving kindness. This may be one of the greatest challenges of our human experiences. Can you be one of these highly conscious, self-actualised people?

"Where there is no love, put love, and you will find love."

St John of the cross.

When we understand and practice this, we have commanded a gracious power within a testing situation, and extended a superpower unto ourselves. In operating using our Elements of Attention, Attraction and Kindness, we can intervene and change not only our own, but other people's outcomes, become peaceful with ourselves, our environment, our fellow humans and our planet. Make this one of your intentions.

To reiterate;
if you only feel Loving kindness then you cannot give out fear.

If you only feel fear then you cannot give out Loving kindness.

Start this today:

Suspend any judgement of others, suspend your own desire to be right when you feel you need to point out the wrong.

Stand aside for someone in the queue behind you who is running late.

Hold the door open at every chance you get, give a smile to the person who never seems to smile.

Buy a coffee for the homeless person you pass each morning.

Look for every opportunity to give away your Loving kindness, especially to those who exhibit fear.

"When you have a choice to be right, or to be kind, choose to be kind."

Wayne. W. Dyer

Finally. Take a moment to consider some Reflections and then write these down:

1. What is one key realisation or reinforcement of your own knowledge of Loving Kindness that you can take away?
2. What could you improve on in your use of the Element of Loving Kindness?
3. How has your past use of the Element of Loving Kindness benefited others and your own wellbeing?

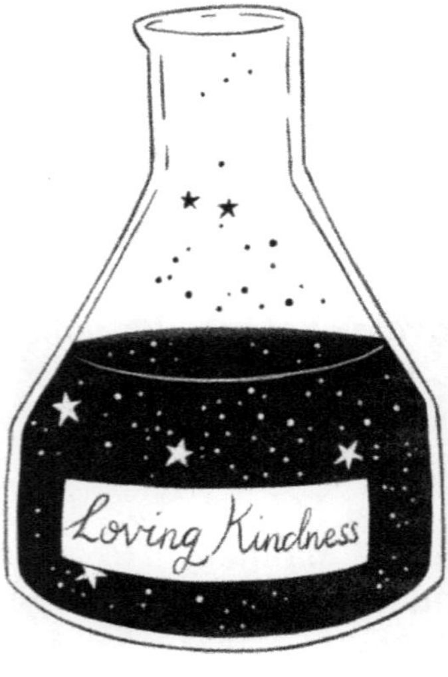
Loving Kindness

Element Ten : Forgiveness

"To forgive is to set a prisoner free and discover that prisoner was you."

Lewis B Smedes

There are many varieties of Forgiveness and many degrees of hurt that require Forgiveness in order to move beyond hurt. But before proceeding further, let me be clear in what I mean by the Element of Forgiveness, specifically what kind of forgiveness is critical to our wellbeing.

For our purposes I will define the Element of Forgiveness as the following. Forgiveness is the act of unreservedly, gracefully and unconditionally letting go of suffering which comes from your own resistance to a wrong done, either by yourself or someone else, against yourself or against someone else, through sufficient relative and genuine understanding of the wrong doer, and the circumstances whether that is yourself or another.

This may seem like a long-winded explanation, but there are many degrees of hurt to cover and often deep complexities in circumstances that would benefit from Forgiveness, ranging from what may be a passing slight, to the extreme of an imprisonable offence. In all of these, Forgiveness will play an enormous part in determining the direction of your life. Forgiveness is not just a matter of saying I forgive, it's a matter of deep and genuine meaning.

Being able to achieve this requires seeing Forgiveness in a whole different light to the one instinctively understood by most. That light in which we see Forgiveness is as an act, foremost of compassion for oneself, and only secondly as an absolution of another's acts. Yet at the same time it must be born out of a genuine release of condemnation.

Forgiveness, like all our Elements In Being holds within it more evidence of the great paradoxes of life. The more I consider the challenges of achieving contentment, the clearer the paradoxical nature of the actions we take to attain contentment becomes. If that were not the case, life would not at times be so challenging. The action and the effect of Forgiveness is one of the clearest examples of these paradox.

Mark Twain summed this up poetically when he said

"Forgiveness is the scent that the violet sheds on the heal that has crushed it."

So, to commence our work on the Element of Forgiveness, it's timely to say that when we, or one of our loved ones, have been wronged or offended, the first two steps to take are:

To be able to fully acknowledge and understand our response.

To be able to fully acknowledge and understand the limitations of the wrong doers' perspective, build up to the offence and the loss that the offence may cause.

I'm not suggesting that what has happened should in any way be condoned or necessarily forgotten, but rather to start with acknowledged and understood.

In a sense, to start to understand Forgiveness, we need to begin to look at the opposites of Forgiveness and what the hidden functions of these opposites are.
When we are unforgiving, there are many different words to describe what we may be feeling or that illustrate a sense of what we want. Words such as blame, resentment, retribution, or punishment become focused in thought and form a perpetuation of our own suffering. They are understandably thoughts and feelings which hold a resistance to what has happened and consequently what now is.

At this point it is useful to highlight a key component central to why Forgiveness is often difficult. This component is some form of loss to, or of, oneself. Not only have we been wronged in some way, but we have a form of resistance to what has happened, what we have now lost. This resistance occurs in many forms, we are all quite unique and so our responses differ also. We may hold grudges, sometimes for decades, anger may erupt or bitterness may fester, we may want retribution, seek pay back or the transgressors may simply become dead to us.

A hidden function of our resistant thoughts and feelings then can be to deny our loss, and thus prevent a process of grief and acceptance to occur. In this light, the unforgiving thoughts and feelings we have can be seen as completely rational. After all, who would want to accept a loss, and the closer the loss is to our heart, the greater the desire can be to hold on to what was, or deny that which is now our reality.

If we think about this further, we can see how the strength of this hidden function could increase as the importance or value of our loss increases. It is easier to forgive being let down by a friend who cancelled the get together and had chosen to meet another friend, than it is to forgive the same friend who had an affair with your partner.

Another hidden function of being unforgiving may be the avoidance of looking at any aspect of ourselves, and our influence or part in the situation. Of course, we may not have a part in it. We may be entirely innocent and separate from what has occurred, but there may be some situations where we cannot forgive, yet there are things we have done, even in an underlying way, which may have contributed to what has happened. In the two examples of our friend who has either betrayed us with their affair, or preference for another friend, our increasing sense of blame or resentment also has the function of preventing us looking inward at ourselves in order to understand any of our own contributing behaviours to the situation. Perhaps we had been increasingly distant and inattentive to our partner, maybe we had become irritable and critical with our friend. If we are absorbed in resentment, then we may well be unable to see these issues, and thus our unforgiving focus has another effect, it prevents us accessing our Element of Reflection.

So, what of forgiveness? If retaining blame and resentment of another maintains so much suffering in ourselves, can Forgiveness really release that suffering?

One way to answer this is to look at suffering itself. Going back to our examples, we can see that the suffering we experience is beyond the physical loss. With our friend who has chosen a preference for meeting someone else rather than ourselves, we may feel let down by their cancellation, but not feel a sense of suffering until we are conscious of their apparent preference for a different friend. Days weeks or even months may pass before we find this out, and it is not until we find out that our suffering starts. We will suffer in the same way to this when we are in physical pain, which can be unbearable when we add our emotional and cognitive resistance to it.

Whether or not you have a current situation in which you could be practicing Forgiveness, you can begin working on Forgiveness yourself.

For the next 24 hours, pay attention to your thoughts of blame or resentment towards either yourself or another. These may be slight or even cause deep suffering, but either way, tune in to these thoughts and notice the feelings that come with them. It doesn't matter if there is only a minimal amount of Forgiveness required, practicing for today is about choosing to be different. So, does this blame or resentment have loss as a part of it? Have you a loss of trust, value, or self-importance?

Each day there can be dozens of reasons to be resentful or offended. Some may be simple, perhaps your coworker criticised you, or the bus didn't stop and drove right by. Maybe the blame you feel is towards yourself, you were late picking up the kids or you yelled at your partner. For this day, try noticing and then asking yourself; do I need to hold on to these thoughts and feelings because of an act which was done from mine or another's momentary, temporary level of consciousness?

By choosing to let go of my offence, my resistance to what has occurred, l am not condoning, but l am acknowledging my resistance to what has happened, and then releasing my suffering. l can now forgive either myself or the other involved. You are positively activating your Elements in Being.

Finally. Take a moment to consider some Reflections and then write these down:
1. What is one key realisation or reinforcement of your own knowledge of Forgiveness that you can take away?
2. What could you improve on in your use of the Element of Forgiveness?
3. How has your past use of the Element of Forgiveness benefited others and your own wellbeing?

Element Eleven : Courage

"Two roads diverged in a yellow wood,
And sorry l could not travel both
And be one traveler, long l stood
And looked down one as far as l could
To where it bent in the undergrowth;

Then took the other, as just as fair,
And having perhaps the better claim,
Because it was grassy and wanted wear;
Though as for that the passing there
Had worn them really about the same,

And both that morning equally lay
In leaves no step had trodden black.
Oh, l kept the first for another day!
Yet knowing how way leads on to way,
l doubted if l should ever come back.

l shall be telling this with a sigh
Somewhere ages and ages hence:
Two roads diverged in a wood, and l —
l took the one less traveled by,
And that has made all the difference."

Robert Frost - The Road Not Taken

When we reach the latter period of our lives, those that have already got there wholeheartedly confirm, that it is the things they have not done that weigh heaviest in their hearts, rather than the things they have done. These are the lost opportunities, the regrets of what could have been rather than what has been. To avert this disaster on occasions both great and small, it is necessary to be bold, fearless and brave, to summon the Element of Courage and seize the moment or the day. I'm not suggesting that you should leap, without a sensible degree of consideration, into whatever new, dangerous or exciting opportunity you may find, but rather that there are a continuous flow of key 'openings' in life that may create a paradigm shift in your physical material journey, as well as your non physical spiritual journey.

It is at these times that fear requires a worthy opponent, and as Nelson Mandela reflected so crucially:

"I learned that Courage was not the absence of fear, but the triumph over it."

I would also assert that Love is a bedfellow of courage in this regard. Imagine not just the famous figures of history who have, with their Courage and Loving Kindness, changed the destiny of themselves and humanity, but the individual common men and women who equally, and unsung have played their part.

Without Courage, all other Elements of our Being may be nothing more than straw dogs. So, as fear is the most dangerous threat to man. Courage, together with Loving kindness is its sword and shield.

Of all the human emotions to overcome, fear and our anxious bodily responses to danger present us with some of our greatest hurdles. Because fear is a protective survival response, bypassing or working in confused tandem with the logical brain, our perspective is narrowed and honed on perceived threats, and our logical rational thinking is often overridden by the urgency our emotions place on this danger. This is a highly effective tool where immediate threat to life exists, but in our modern lives fear is generally disproportionate and not aligned to any real existential threat to our immediate survival.

We are persistently exposed to subjective, multi-level fears or threats through our conditioned life which creates particularly negative impacts on our general anxiety levels.

It is a life born of an overprotected and risk averse culture that prevents us from learning how to normalise uncertainty. Additionally, we have a culture that celebrates overblown Egos whether on a personal, group, community, religious, race or national level. The Ego's perspective of entitlement, competition and attachment to a sense of self and image is consistently reinforced through formats such as technology, social media, news, tv and advertising. At the same time Egos feel threatened by these very sources that promote Egoism in the form of comparison, competition self-promotion and subsequent disconnection.

As you consider fear in your life, it is crucial to see it not just in terms of individual threats and fears, but in layers and layers of multiple fears which incrementally, persistently and incessantly gnaw away at your sense of peace and contentment. In a consumer and target driven society where success is measured and rewarded by fame, growth, key performance indicators, status, appearances, "likes" and material possessions, the subtle fears which grow and form are born of perceived micro failures that can turn into an underlying sense of ultimate threat, damaging your own self love, self worth and self belief. These are as dangerous as any dark alley on a late night walk home, not as immediate, but highly more pervasive.

Fear has a multitude of facets. It can be a form of control of others, a protector against genuine danger, a hidden influencer of our behaviours and a quicksand into which our thinking can sink where the more we struggle, the greater the pull downwards. All of the Elements in our being interact with fear but no matter what the specific fear, with Courage and Loving kindness, it can be overcome by embracing the fear yet still choosing to act.

As we travel this mortal coil, with a continuously opening blank canvas on which to paint a limitless variety of memories, the most vibrant, luminous memories will be those that have harnessed the power found through employing the highest degrees of Courage and Loving Kindness. This is because our most pure and genuine sense of self is displayed when we act with Courage and Loving Kindness. It is our Courage in the act of collecting these memories that allows us to self-actualise the richness of our Being.

Being courageous requires rather a lot doesn't it. Love for something greater than the fear, faith in ourselves, tolerance of uncertainty and of the unknown, acceptance of potential loss, and a degree of hope in a new potential. Though it doesn't mean being ignorant of risk and not acting to mitigate it.

Courage in facing danger is generally the act of Courage that first comes to mind when we use the word, but I invite you to consider that it is the daily use of Courage more broadly to action and navigate towards our dreams which strides us out to our own destiny:

"All our dreams may come true, if we have the Courage to pursue them."
Walt Disney

Moral Courage is particularly important. To be courageous enough to stand firm on moral ground when those around you threaten, intimidate, or appose is a strength often exceeding the trials of physical Courage.

To build Courage in your life, begin with allowing yourself a few moments to consider what things you avoid doing, even though there are no physical restrictions. These may be as varied as relatively simple daily matters, right through to classic 'jumping out of a plane' type avoidances.

Write these out as goals to test out as behavioural experiments. With one of the activities avoided, consider what you fear may happen if you do it, and how much do you believe that thought?

Now consider any different outcomes which may occur, no matter how little you believe them? Make your plan, think about the steps you will take to move towards your avoided fear. Break this down and consider the full build up to the action and exactly how you're going to do it. Picture in your minds eye going through the whole event and stay with any anxiety this may produce. Don't try to distract your mental image, just notice that this creates feelings with corresponding negative fearful thoughts. These thoughts and feelings want to feed one another, that's the fear getting in the way. You may question or judge yourself in being able to do this, acknowledge these are only thoughts born from your anxious perspective. Stay with this until you start to feel calmer. You may wish to repeat this exercise before you actually commence your challenge and grow your courage.

When you are ready to practice for real, then you may begin with a remembering that combining your Element of Courage with the intention of

Loving kindness for whatever happens is the key to success. Be courageous and rare:

"Even the most courageous among us only rarely has the courage to face what he already knows."
Friedrich Nietzsche

Once you have completed your experiment to action your avoided behaviour, ask yourself how your thoughts before hand match up to what actually happened, and additionally, how do you now feel?

Now that you have begun actively developing your Element of Courage, don't stop with one experiment. Consider other avoided opportunities that become available to you, and implement the same practice. The more you do this, the greater the momentum to eliminating regret in your final years.

"Carpe Diem." (seize the day)
Book 1, Odes – Horace (23BC)

Finally. Take a moment to consider some Reflections and then write these down:
1. What is one key realisation or reinforcement of your own knowledge of Courage that you can take away?
2. What could you improve on in your use of the Element of Loving Kindness?
3. How has your past use of the Element of Courage changed yours and others destiny?

Element Twelve : Belief

"The moment you doubt whether you can fly, you cease for ever to be able to do it."

Peter Pan. J.M.Barrie.

A belief itself is not necessarily a truth, but a thought that has grown from repeatedly thinking, into a heartfelt sense of what is simply right. As you consider your Beliefs in this chapter, tune into both your simple and your highly complex Beliefs. No matter what their complexity, they have an absolute power over both your reality and your destiny.

Through our ageing and growing experience, we form our beliefs that standing alone, can be either extremely restorative or damaging. They are important Elements In Being because, despite the fact that they may not be necessarily true, their effect can be just as powerful as if they are true.

From the point of view of our well-being, this is a vital piece of information, because if you cast your mind back to what is so necessary in the Element of Attraction, you may recall that you need to attract, not only from the head, but also from the heart. What this means is that, if we whole heartedly believe, then this feeds directly, into what we attract.

The critical effects of these thoughts becoming Beliefs is fundamentally either that the positive Belief acts as a placebo, or the negative Belief acts as a nocebo. To put it another way, when we believe, our body chemistry matches up to that Belief, and provides a change in our internal environment to facilitate the movement towards the outcome of that belief. Once we truly understand the absolute integration of our thoughts, feelings and behaviours, the evidence for the physical effects of Belief will become visible to us in ever increasing ways. The other major problem, is that when our belief is creating the nocebo, rather than placebo effect, then it will be detrimental to our wellbeing. The difference between placebo and nocebo is that placebo is the belief we have what we need to achieve our desired outcome, whereas nocebo is the Belief we don't have what we need to achieve our desired outcome. Either way, the stronger our wholehearted Belief is, the more likely we are to move towards that Belief.

The old saying "Be careful what you wish for, it might come true" should really be changed to "Be careful what you believe, it might come true"

Beliefs are not without problems. They can tend to become rigid. As a Belief is formed, a bias starts to occur towards that Belief and this reduces our open mindedness. So, we are all believers to greater or lesser extents, whether they be the simplest or most complex beliefs, or the tiniest or grandest philosophies, even if those beliefs are of nothing, they are still a Belief, and we come to our beliefs in many varied ways. Spontaneously they may appear in the assembly of connected thoughts and notions, or subtly they may creep up on us over decades. Our beliefs can be wildly vague or complex and intricate, deeply experiential.

In the melting pot which is the formation of beliefs, the roll of the dice also brings options in the development of your Beliefs that are beyond your control. When you were born, who your parents are, where you live, who you come across in your daily existence, these are the kind of daily circumstances that are granted to us, influencing and repeating our thoughts into beliefs, which ultimately are just thoughts that we keep thinking.

We may have not been open or aware enough to question our beliefs, but if we are determined and up for a challenge, eventually we can create a mind that is brave and conscious enough to question and evaluate our thoughts, and in turn our beliefs, then consequently allow ourselves the unrestricted freedom for beliefs to ebb and flow in such a way that they beneficially fulfil our needs rather than hold us hostage to their power.

One of the great guiding principles that threads through this book, acting as a rule for wellbeing, is to have a mind that is open to everything and attached nowhere. Beliefs themselves, if we are not honestly open and reflective can themselves establish a barrier to our openness. The reason having an open mind is so important is that it does not limit possibility. In being open and unattached to ideas, our options are limitless, and at the same time any judgement is negated. Once we are held captive by our beliefs, we may become disconnected from others, liable to criticise and be criticised, become defensive and to justify. We will gravitate toward those of similar views and beliefs who will readily reinforce our own and so too theirs.

To illustrate the progress of thoughts into beliefs we can imagine that at the outset, we are sat at the top of a mountain. From our vantage point high up at the peak, we can see clearly the different aspects of the mountain, each side, each facet, represents an alternative school of thought or belief. All can be compared and viewed with equal perspective, yet the detail of the ridges, cliffs and rocks can only be seen with movement closer towards these faces. But then, as you are taking in the view of all 360 degrees, something happens, it could be pure accident, or something more alluring, maybe the wind blows hard, and to avoid this, you seek shelter walking down from the top to the calmer slopes of the mountain. Or you see something that takes your fancy lower down a particular slope, the sun is shining there on the rocks and looks warm and inviting. As you move from the top, your perspective has now shifted, the view you have alters in your new vantage point, and no longer reveals the opposite side of the mountain. Your view of this side now is enhanced, you notice in more detail the grain of the rock, the worn path of previous occupants. The further down you go, the more intimately you see this side, and at the same time, the further hidden the opposite side is. So, to use this analogy with our perspective of belief, it would take quite an effort to shift away from what is in our attention and our established belief, to walk around or back, up and then down, to the other side of the mountain. Not only that, but you have formed a connection with this aspect of the mountain. It has a familiarity, and a present reality that includes you. In the same way, beliefs become a part of us, an important aspect of our identity. Changing or challenging them can be like climbing back up a mountain to get to a place we don't want to go, when we feel that we are already in the right place.

Beliefs are so important to us that we must absolutely pay attention to them, and constantly be open to challenge what they are and where they take us. They are our guidance system for our intention, and our intention becomes our destiny.

Now as the exploration of our Elements draws to a close, we must consider how powerful the Element of Belief is. The formation of a belief is also the attempted fulfilment of our need to rid our minds of uncertainty, yet it does not give us true certainty. Therefore, it is vital that we become comfortable in the presence of uncertainty if we are to reduce our dependency on the negative impacts of Belief.

If Belief is so fraught with problems, and yet an indelible mark in our being, how can we harness the positive potentials it can bring, such as the incredible physical changes caused through the placebo effect, or the guidance it brings towards positive intentions? This comes down to the deeper underlying feeling that comes with belief, that of Faith and Trust. If we can have faith and trust in matters which do not have absolute certainty, with the acknowledgement and acceptance that, as humans, there is a limit to what we can know, then we have truly conquered our greatest challenge, and at the same time opened ourselves up to the benefits of the unfolding universe.

So, in essence Belief is everything, yet at the same time, nothing. Being too attached to beliefs, being shielded from the opposite sides of the mountain is a destiny with reduced options and control. *"Have a mind that's open to everything, and attached nowhere."* Wander all the mountainsides of your life, gaze in awe on what you discover and tell about it, but don't get attached. Then when you return to the top of the mountain, you will truly know it and your place on it for the very first time.

For this final Element, take some time to consider your own beliefs that may have been challenged by others, or where your bias has kept you from objectively exploring the alternatives to your beliefs. It may have been something simple, a debate about the performance of one of the players in the sports game, or the generalisation of a person in a particular group. A homeless woman in the shop doorway, or the hooded teenager loitering in the street. Some of the subjects in this book may also be a challenge to your beliefs. Perhaps as you raise the awareness of them you may challenge the beliefs you have of yourself.

To round off the Element of Belief we must again practically apply ourselves, this time to discover more of this Element as it exists within ourselves.

The Danish philosopher Soren Kierkegaard said:

"Once you label me, you negate me."

Or to rephrase this; when you name something, you define that something in such a way that all other possible definitions are excluded. You put a boundary up which restricts possibility and denies other aspects of reality.

When you label something you also define yourself as someone who needs to label, and in a sense, judge. For example, if I say you are a Father, I do not include that you are also a Son, and might also be a Brother, a friend, a worker, a tennis player, a philosopher, an artist, etc. Or, if I said you were a gossip, I do not mention that perhaps you are a Mother, a listener, a person who is loving and kind.

Your beliefs are a series of labels that you live your life by. How are they negating you, your life and any or all of your connections?

Are your beliefs facts or truths? Of course they are not facts, otherwise you wouldn't call them beliefs.

Socrates applied a test to anyone approaching him with rumours and commentary, or what we might call labels. The test involved answering yes to at least one of the three questions below.

Let's apply Socrates test of three to your beliefs, those labels about yourself, the people in your life and your future:
Write out three negative beliefs you have on the subjects below:

One label or Belief about myself:

One label or Belief about others (friends, family, colleagues):

One label or Belief I have about my past:

One label or belief I have about my present:

One label or belief I have about my future:

Now let's put them to the following Socratic test of three.

The first test is of Truth. Have you made absolutely sure that what you believe is true?

The second test is of Goodness.
Is what you believe something good?

The third test is of Usefulness.
Is what you believe going to be useful to you?

If your Belief does not pass one of these three tests, Socrates would then conclude;
"If what you believe is neither true, good or useful, why believe it at all?"

Now go back to your answers and question how much you believe each of them either one way or another? Ask yourself; just because I believe this, does it make it true?

Can you challenge your own thinking and find another way of looking at your thoughts altogether?

Take a moment to consider some Reflections and then write these down:
1. What is one key realisation or reinforcement of your own knowledge of Belief that you can take away?
2. What could you improve on in your use of the Element of Belief?
3. How has your past use of the Element of Belief benefited others and your own wellbeing?

If you have stuck with me so far on this elemental

journey, congratulations, I know you have the building blocks for a more meaningful, content life. To get to this requires persistent action too, which you will already have begun by putting into practice the tasks at the end of each Element. Understanding alone will not change how you feel for very long. Actively working on the insights you are developing of yourself is vital to create deeper, lasting change, so maintain your practice. Over time you will notice that both you and the people around you will become more content, more supportive, more peaceful and loving.

Chapter Six
Implementation

From learning to practice

"You can't cross the sea merely by standing and staring at the water."
Rabindranath Tagore

The key components required to enhance each of the Elements are:

Building our understanding.
Planning and practicing your Elements with a deliberateness.
Creating a place of stillness.
Paying attention.
Noticing the effect on Ego.
Staying with and embracing what is.
Moving on with our new behaviour.
Reflecting on how our thoughts and feelings change in line with our behaviour.

Now it's time to start implementing your learnings, but before we start, and while it is fresh in your mind, let's look at your beliefs for a moment. There are degrees of Belief which assist us to, or prevent us from, moving forward. These vary from total disbelief, to being utterly convinced. Where do you sit with your belief of what you have read? I am sure that there will be many points which you are sceptical about, or that you might even disagree with. Naturally, any scepticism may increase the barriers to commencing the practical section of your journey. But it is this practical component which will offer you the greatest opportunity for confirming, challenging or changing your beliefs. If you ever want to fully understand, then you must experience. So, for now, if you are serious about change, then you must willingly suspend any disbelief. Let's imagine you are about to commence watching the latest science fiction fantasy movie. You wouldn't enjoy the film if you doubted every imagined creature or process....

"Beam me up Scotty."

Practicing your Elements In Being is a daily focus. It will play an ongoing and ever-present role in your routine, and creates movement towards contentment and inner peace. Consequently, the following affirmations are your basic platform for change. Along with understanding, they form the firm foundations on which a lasting actualising self can manifest.

The schedule I have created is not entirely rigid, in that you may wish to vary it to your life situation. If you deviate appropriate to your own circumstances, this won't mean you have failed. However, the order in which Elements are practiced, and the repetition and growth of them has been created to link together in the most natural way, and to flow more easily for you. There will be days and times when you are not able to follow the plan, such is the way of life. In these times simply remind yourself that it is ok, and you will recommence the next day you are ready.

The day before you start your first practice, it is important to do some planning as well as to make a commitment to yourself that you will keep these times sacred to you. There are three crucial points to each day which must be ring-fenced and protected for a sole purpose; the pure implementation of your Elements In Being. Decide beforehand at what specific times you will do these. They are 3 separate periods of 10 minutes each, the first and last of which are within 30 minutes of waking, and within 30 minutes of sleeping. The remaining 10 minute period should be timed to fit within a natural mid-day break, when you are likely having your lunch break. Each one of these three provides different benefits:

The first is a priming, calibrating point that will set you on a positive course for your day. Each day at this point your focus will be based on one of a list of 22 affirmations that use either a single or selected combination of the Elements In your Being.

The second midway point provides a grounding point with the Elements of Attention and Connection. This key junction in your day serves to put a distance from the routine, noise and action of your ordinary commitments. Put simply, this is a time for bringing back your present moment Attention and re-Connection with the extraordinary, both internally and externally... It is a space to BE.

The third point at the end of your day is a space

for reflection and reminder of your daily morning affirmation. A time to look at the relevant aspects of your day that line up with your affirmation, as well as a preparation for your sleep. The thoughts running through your mind at this point are like the ingredients of a marinade in which your mind will sit over the next 7 hours or so. Making your life "taste" good requires paying attention to the quality and balance of these "ingredients."

These 30 minutes of time, broken into three, will become the anchor for your Being in the ocean of life. As you manage the trials and tribulations of daily dramas, these points are there for you as steadfast supports to return to.

At the start and end of each day, your time is spent following the same process. This is designed to best prepare you for the day ahead and for sleep, as well as to build a habitual pattern, making the process easier over time. Critically for success though, you must deliberately put yourself before all else in your application of these 30 minutes. Remember, the actualisation of you is the most important thing here, even if you believe that other responsibilities or people are more important. To neglect your own priority for these brief periods will deny both others and yourself the best version of you.

And so, to begin...

Morning and evening :

Blending your Elements In Being

Find your quiet spot, and take a few moments to become still, and clear your thoughts before you start.

Now, slowly read through the introduction to your daily affirmation in the following pages. Next leave a small space in time and then repeat your "I am" affirmations slowly three times, leaving a slow deep breath in and out between each recital.

These affirmations are designed to first reinforce your Elements of Being, and secondly to guide your attraction to the attributes of a self-actualised Being; Abraham Maslow, the American Psychologist and creator of the hierarchy of needs theory, viewed achieving these qualities as being evidence that a person has attained the highest level of who they can be. To truly activate these statements, proceed with a commitment in your own mind to implement a deliberate, practical application of each statement. Each one of these requires the conscious use of one or more of your Elements In Being.

Day one affirmation - I am Reflection.

Revisit a situation or difficult encounter from yesterday or earlier today in which you would like to have made a better response. Use an observing eye on yourself, as if you are a spectator looking down upon your own experience as well as other people involved.

Notice your feelings as you participated in the event.

What thought is attached to that feeling?

What is the feeling trying to say?

What did the situation cause in you?

How did your responses influence what took place?

Did you have a resistance or unease to the situation within your inner thoughts, feelings and subsequent behaviours?

Acknowledge it for what it is – no judgement needed.

What was in your control?

What was outside your control?

What did you influence, what message did you send to others because of the the way you were?

Confirm, whatever happened is all that could happen based on the level of consciousness of all those involved at that moment in time.

Now affirm out loud: "I am Reflection."

Slowly breathe in, breathe out. Repeat twice more.

Day two affirmation - I am Attention.

Take a moment to realise your own Attention. In this space, regard yourself, the essence of you, as separate from your body. See yourself from this unencumbered perspective without physical identity. What you are without the skin and bone, the labels and statuses that are seen by yourself and others in the physical world. Your pure awareness, your pure Attention is bringing this and every other exact, unique moment into existence.

Remove the labels and names of what comes to your attention. Simply hear, see, smell, feel and experience what is, without attachment to a definition. You may hear the clock ticking, a dog barking, the tree swaying, but begin to let go of these labels and notice they are all part of the whole interacting within the whole.

Remind yourself that without your Attention this present moment's unique attributes would not exist because your attention is an integral part of the whole.

Now affirm out loud: "I am Attention."
Slowly breathe in, breathe out. Repeat twice more.

Day three affirmation - I am Dreaming.

Starting by becoming still and quiet. Listen to the sound of silence. There is a pitch of noise that is silence and always sits there in the background, mostly unnoticed, but always available to us. Tune into this sound of silence as the channel for your Dreaming. As you do so, allow your mind to wander into the spontaneous creations of unencumbered and boundary-less realms. Put your attention deep within, allowing, without a need to interpret or understand what appears. Notice only that your Dreaming is the miraculous appearance in this moment. You are the creator, without an attachment or definitions. Take a moment to imagine you have objectified your dreams, and from this place be astonished at their wonder.

Become the power of your dreaming, and know that their creative force will form the basis for manifestations in your life. Remember, what underlies the material is the dream.

Now close your eyes and affirm in your mind:
"I am Dreaming."
Slowly breathe in, breathe out. Repeat twice more.

Day four affirmation - I am Connection.

All things are connected and held together by energy frequency and vibration. Practice your connection to the vibration of sound with a pre-chosen and personally uplifting piece of music. Tune in to the flow of connection:

Find a comfortable space. If you are inside close your eyes as you begin to listen to the music. If you are lucky enough to be outside on a quiet sunny day, raise your eyes to the sky as you tune in to the sound. Put your attention into your own internal space, and visualise the sounds as they travel through those spaces as well as the material of each cell and atom within your body, resonating, reverberating, and for the moments they travel through, influencing and holding each in the musical vibrations captivating grasp. Allow each tiny part of your body to be overcome and controlled by the sounds you hear.

Sing out loud or in your head. Let your body sway to the beat or stir your soul. Allow the hairs to rise on the back of your neck, and your stomach to sense its own void. When the music is done... stay silent for a few minutes staying with the lingering feelings that have run through and connected with you. It is in reality a connection with the flow of spirit which moves through the soul. Everything has a vibration, and music is a pure and deliberate human version of it.

Now affirm out loud: "I am Connection."
Slowly breathe in, breathe out. Repeat twice more.

Day five affirmation – I am Attraction.

Your affirmations are already starting to activate your Element of Attraction. That's the purpose of them.

To Develop Attraction further, visualise yourself going about your day today.

Know that everything you are going to interact with has the quality of a mirror. All your thoughts and heart felt feelings, let's call these emissions, are reflected and multiplied back to you, creating your world. Be conscious how this applies to others too, so that not only are you attracting your own emissions, but so are others.

No matter what you consistently think, feel in your heart and subsequently do is ultimately what you will attract.

It's down to you.

Now affirm out loud: "I am Attraction."
Slowly breathe in, breathe out. Repeat twice more.

Day Six affirmation – I am Meaning.

As you prepare for your affirmation and the day ahead, remember that discovering your Meaning in life will not always be obvious.

On many occasions Meaning will be hidden in suffering, therefore your task will be to value what is, so that you can value what isn't.

If you are in pain, the meaning is to allow you to value non-pain.
If you are grieving, it is to value the lost.
If you are sad it is to value joy.
Without allows us to value with.

Ultimately then, having found the meaning allows us to give it away.

As we become wise through our meanings, we can impart wisdom to others.

Repeat out loud: "I am Meaning."
Slowly breathe in, breathe out. Repeat twice more.

Day seven affirmation – I am Intention

Take a few minutes before you recite your affirmations to think about what you would like to be doing by the time you have habitualised all 22 of them.

Take out a pen and paper and write down this intention;

Be as specific as you can deciding how you will measure your movement towards the intention. Make it achievable and make it relevant to your Meaning.

Imagine what you will be thinking, feeling and doing when you have reached the peaceful contentment of attaining this Intention.

Read back through your descriptions several times to start to commit these to your subconscious then allow them the space to be without attachment to when they will materialise.

Repeat out loud: "I am Intention."
Slowly breathe in, breathe out. Repeat twice more.

Day eight affirmation – I am Gratitude

Consider a person who is, or has been, in your life that you are thankful for. A soul who has helped to make you the person you are. What in particular are you grateful for that this person has brought to you? Visualise them standing in front of you, and either out loud or in your mind, thank them for what they have given you.

Next consider the miraculous yet basic needs that you have met every day, and may normally just take for granted, such as food, water, a home, fresh air, your clothes. Acknowledge your Gratitude.

Finally, choose one part of yourself for which you would desperately miss if you no longer had the benefit that it provides. This could be anything from your eyes, your balance or your memory to your hands, your sense of humour or your taste buds. Again, acknowledge your Gratitude.

Repeat out loud: "I am Gratitude."
Slowly breathe in, breathe out. Repeat twice more.

Day nine affirmation – I am Loving Kindness

As you prepare for today's affirmation, you could do worse than looking at why a lack of Loving Kindness is so negative. If Loving Kindness is missing, then so too are our positive connections. Fear, resentment and judgement will have taken the place of this vital Element and with that a separation from the beneficial use of our other Elements In Being. This causes a deleterious effect on our physical and mental health.

In your interactions today, undertake a deliberate experiment, and suspend any judgement of others. Suspend your own desire to be right when you feel you need to point out the wrong. Choose to be the embodiment of Loving kindness instead. Give up your seat on the bus or train to someone who might need it. Give your neighbour, peer or boss a genuine smile when you see them today. Think of giving away something that you can do without, but that someone else really needs. Step aside for someone behind you in the queue who is running late.

Don't speed up and cross to the opposite side of the road to avoid the homeless person you pass each morning. Buy them a coffee instead, or just silently send your compassion. Look for every opportunity to give away your Loving kindness, especially to those who exhibit fear.

Recite out loud: "I am Loving Kindness."
Slowly breathe in, breathe out. Repeat twice more.

Day ten affirmation – I am Forgiveness.

Begin this affirmation with a reflection of any current or previous suffering that you or a loved one has, or is enduring. Think of who you see as having caused this suffering, whether that is yourself or someone else.

Now fully acknowledge and understand your response to this suffering.

Next fully acknowledge and understand that a "wrong doers" level of consciousness at the time of their actions was determined by everything that they had experienced up until that moment. Their actions were essentially all they were capable of at that time. This is true for us all. In doing this you are not condoning bad action, but releasing your suffering.

Remember that the Element of Forgiveness is the act of unreservedly letting go with grace of the suffering you hold within you. This suffering comes from your own resistance to a real or perceived wrong that has been done or to a loss.

Repeat out loud: "I am Forgiveness."
Slowly breathe in, breathe out. Repeat twice more.

Day eleven affirmation – I am Courage

Today, as you prepare for Courage, consider some of the routine behaviours you have that show you are avoiding your use of this Element. It is the small behaviours we have, or often absence of responses that we give to others, that set up the direction of our lives and how people treat us.

In your day today, become aware of the way others treat you and what you accept or tolerate from them. It's so easy to sit on our Courage, and instead of using it, we tolerate behaviours from others that simply teach that person that they may treat us in an unreasonable way. If this occurs, summon your Courage when you see it and very politely but with absolute clarity let them know this is not acceptable.

Notice also what you have a habit of avoiding. Deliberately challenging your avoidance behaviours, no matter how small, is one gradual and effective way to increase your Courage.

Repeat out loud: "I am Courage."
Slowly breathe in, breathe out. Repeat twice more.

Day twelve affirmation – I am Belief

Belief, it's nothing yet it is everything. What you choose to believe becomes your reality, whether it is real or not. So, the objective of your affirmation today is to open up your Element of Belief to the greater view and in so doing, create a grander reality.

For today, experiment with a deliberately open view of the world. Detach yourself from dogma, opinions and culture. Bring some flexibility to your own beliefs too. Just for today, loosen them and stretch them to see what you could include and what you are missing out on.

Beliefs that are too rigid will act like a tall mountain to shield your view of the other sides. As you climb the mountain, your increasingly broad view will allow you to see all the things your previously rigid beliefs had obscured.

Be kind to yourself with this challenging task, after all Belief has one of the strongest connections to the sense you have of your own individual identity, and consequently will be one of the hardest Elements to recalibrate.

Repeat out loud: "I am Belief."
Slowly breathe in, breathe out. Repeat twice more.

Day thirteen affirmation –
I am an appreciator of beauty

For this affirmation you will need to apply the Elements of Attention and Gratitude.

This can be done in a myriad of ways. As simply as taking a moment on the way out of your front door today to just look up at the sky. Observe the beauty of the clouds as they change shape and glide across the sky. Are they white, silver or dark? Is the sun shining through them casting beams of light on your face from over 90 million miles away?

You could stop for a few long moments by a tree, put your hand out and feel the bark. Notice the miracle that has been created from an invisible force and a tiny seed.

Notice that Beauty can be found everywhere if you take the time to see it, even in the ordinary and ugly.

Repeat out loud: "I am an appreciator of beauty."
Slowly breathe in, breathe out. Repeat twice more.

Day fourteen affirmation – I am on purpose.

To become on purpose, you will need to apply the Elements of Attention, Intention, Meaning and Attraction.

Bring to mind the legacy you will leave behind, the what that you will be remembered for because you have been living "on purpose". What is your Meaning in your gift to the world? This is not your ambition, but the deeper value underlying it.

Your purpose cannot be found in the grandiose, in fact it is necessary for it to be sourced in the daily scintilla of your unique presence. Your ultimate purpose is not a future outcome but the present. Bring this idea into mind as a clear visualisation, acted out preparedly with as much detail as you can muster.

Next, confirm to yourself that no matter what happens today, there is a purpose within and this is part of what's needed just for you. You may not know immediately what that purpose is, but just understanding that it has a purpose for you means eventually, at some point, that purpose will appear.

Finally, remember to pay Attention to what you think, feel in your heart and subsequently do, as this is what you attract.

Repeat out loud: "I am on purpose."
Slowly breathe in, breathe out. Repeat twice more.

Day fifteen affirmation –
I am a resistor of enculturation.

To apply this, you will need to use the Elements of Attention, Loving Kindness, Courage and Belief.

Enculturation is a safety trap which you are drawn into out of your inherent need for belonging. Therefore, pay Attention to all the small and large features of your society, that subtly or overtly make you adjust to fit in and, in so doing, make you lose an important part of your character.

Living without conformity to culture doesn't require holding a lesser view of those who do conform, but it does require Courage and a consciousness of the labels and boxes a culture imposes on the individuals who live within it, as well as challenging your own Beliefs. Whilst culture provides a sense of belonging, it also creates a reason to judge those who don't conform, leading to a loss of Loving Kindness and excludes anything beyond the label.

As Soren Kierkegaard said;

"Once you label me, you negate me."

Repeat out loud: "I am a resistor of enculturation." Slowly breathe in, breathe out. Repeat twice more.

Day sixteen affirmation –
I am welcome to the unknown.

Here you will need to apply the Elements of Belief, Courage and Dreaming.

In this state, your Beliefs may well be tested, and need to be adjusted as you venture into different experiences, and garner new revelations. You will invoke Courage to actively embrace the fear of the unknown, and seek out the opportunities within this change. Courage will maintain your progress despite any sense of threat or of feeling afraid of the future.

The unknown, which comprises uncertainty is the fuel for worry, yet when it is mastered and tamed, the unknown becomes the window through which Dreaming can appear. This Dreaming window is your interface with the unknown where you can cultivate the fresh and exciting from your open curiosity.

Repeat out loud: "I am welcome to the unknown."
Slowly breathe in, breathe out. Repeat twice more.

Day seventeen affirmation - I am highly enthusiastic.

This will require applying the Elements of Attention, Intention, Meaning and Belief.

If you are operating with enthusiasm, you must be "on purpose". By this definition you must be living with Attention, Intention, Meaning and Belief in your actions. To become highly enthusiastic requires activating these four key Elements.

Whether you are a taxi driver in Baghdad or a lawyer in L.A, the title you have matters not to the level of enthusiasm you choose, but the meaning you find in your work is essential. When we experience someone who is highly enthusiastic, we enter a realm beyond the ordinary. Imagine a taxi driver who tells you on first meeting you that they have a choice of music for you to listen to on your journey. A beverage to drink, and even a variety of newspapers to read. They are well presented with shiny shoes and get out to open the door for you with a friendly greeting. How does this experience make you feel and how does it make the taxi driver feel? Enthusiasm is infectious and is about wanting to get the maximum out of the present moment, it is accelerated with Intention and is borne of the Meaning behind the action.

Repeat out loud: "I am highly enthusiastic."
Slowly breathe in, breathe out. Repeat twice more.

Day eighteen affirmation – I am inner in my direction.

There is a similarity to day fifteen when you practiced "I am a resistor of enculturation" because both affirmations are focused on being true to yourself. Therefore, you will again need to apply the Elements of Attention, Loving Kindness, Courage and Belief.

To move towards an inner direction today, you will need to listen (pay Attention) to the voice within, and direct your thoughts and actions by your own moral values and Beliefs, as opposed to those of others or external norms. This requires Courage with and Loving Kindness towards others, regardless of their contrary positions.

Repeat out loud: "I am inner in my direction,"
Slowly breathe in, breathe out. Repeat twice more.

Day nineteen affirmation -
I am detached from outcome.

This will require the application of your Elements of Attention, Meaning and Gratitude.

An outcome is in the future, it is not now. Therefore focusing your Attention on the present moment will immediately assist you in detaching from outcomes. Alone, this cannot prevent an attachment to outcome, as it is impossible for Human Beings to always have their Attention in the present moment.

The major pitfall of being attached to outcomes is the loss of the present which comes as a result. In addition to this, an antagonistic relationship also develops with events that occur in "the now" that seem to get in the way of your intended outcome. Here you will need to bring in the Elements of Meaning and Gratitude. When the Meaning of any roadblocks to outcomes can be found then your antagonism will dissipate. If you can then invoke Gratitude for these roadblocks, not only will you thankfully embrace the benefits of what has occurred, but you will increase your openness to everything.

As your day progresses examine any strong attachments you may have to future plans, then contemplate that what occurs in each moment of today, (and every other day as it occurs) has and will be your most important outcome.

Repeat out loud: "I am detached from outcome,"
Slowly breathe in, breathe out. Repeat twice more.

Day twenty affirmation -
I am independent of the good opinion of others.

This will require the application of your Elements of Connection, Belief, Loving Kindness and Forgiveness.

Here you have the freedom to make Connection to your true self. Period. Being independent of the good opinion of others is not synonymous with being unkind or thoughtless about people. In fact, it is caring about who a person truly is.

This affirmation is essentially the same as the Yoga mantra Sat Naam, meaning; truth is my essence or I am truth, in the Sikh language. What you are doing with this affirmation is actualising your true identity as an infinite being in human form, regardless of someone else's thoughts, or often what you may think are their thoughts. In so doing you are also allowing the other person to become their own truth. This is a display of unconditional Loving Kindness......and wow, it's freeing for all concerned.

You cannot control others, but you can control how you feel about them and Forgive them, therefore if you can find peace within yourself as you interact with even the most difficult people, you will be free. Enjoy your independence from the good opinion of others

Repeat out loud: "I am independent of the good opinion of others."
Slowly breathe in, breathe out. Repeat twice more.

Day twenty-one affirmation -
I am without the need to exert control over others.

Following your work yesterday, today's affirmation becomes much easier. It requires the Elements of Connection, Belief, Loving Kindness and Attraction.

The focus on valuing the truth and unique essence of who you are, of being yourself, and the consciousness you have developed of your independence, also allows a shift in any desires to control others independence. Paradoxically, this increases your positive Connection with others.

It's time to deliberately notice these desires, subtle or otherwise, in order to curb them. As you practice this affirmation, be conscious of managing your Beliefs. Experiment by holding back on your need to influence, correct or argue with others views. Instead simply watch, listen, send Loving Kindness and reflect back how you hadn't thought of something in that way.

Notice how you may judge and see others behaviours. Observe your own need to control, but without acting on any thoughts to do so. As you do this you will take active control of your Element of Attraction supporting positive rather than negative Connection.

Repeat out loud: "I am without the need to exert control over others."
Slowly breathe in, breathe out. Repeat twice more.

Day twenty-two affirmation -
I am connected with all living things as truly and immediately as I am with myself.

This will require application of your Elements of Connection, Attention, Loving Kindness and Gratitude.

As our series of affirmations draws to a close, the most fundamental lesson to reinforce is that of unity and equity with all. It is hard not to see ourselves as separate, yet it is in experiencing with Gratitude and Loving Kindness our Connection to all living things that we unify the soul.

As you embark today on a deliberate plan to do this, use all of your Attention as if you have 360-degree senses. Deploy particular awareness to the co-existence, co-dependence and interactions of all, including yourself as parts of an integrated whole.

Repeat out loud: "I am connected with all living things as truly and immediately as I am with myself."

Slowly breathe in, breathe out. Repeat twice more.

Midday affirmation - I am

Quite simply, at the mid point of your day, your affirmation is to just be. This means using your Attention and Connection without interpretation. Where possible, include in your lunch break going out on a deliberately slow walk or to sit in a place of nature where you can experience fresh air, gardens, trees, plants or better still a park. Take your footwear off too, if you can.

Eliminate distractions and make sure you leave your phone at home, the car or work. Deliberately decide to use all your focus as practiced with the Element of Attention.

Take a slow and deep breath focusing on the sensation of the air entering your lungs, your body and the oxygen entering your bloodstream.

As each breath occurs, your energy and alertness increases.

Hold each breath comfortably for a few seconds, and then slowly exhale, again feeling the air as it leaves your body. Repeat this, three times, each time followed by the affirmation "I am".

Next, turn your attention to your thoughts. Have they drifted to somewhere, something, or sometime beyond this moment? If so, return your attention to the moment you are in, let them go with the permission that you will consider them once you have returned to your post lunch tasks. Use your senses to anchor yourself to the moment you are in.

Notice that you feel sensations against your body and internally, the sounds near and distant. See the patterns and colours of nature and man-made constructions, the light, the shapes. Continue to pay attention to any thoughts that arise and allow them to go if they are not of the now. As you do so, let go of the need to label and interpret what you witness. Simply pay Attention with an accepting mind and ask yourself "Who is the 'I' that is witnessing this moment?"

Observe the attention itself that comes through you and acknowledge that there is only this moment.

I now invite you to reflect on what you have learned about yourself, what has changed and how you can continue to keep the Elements In your Being active.

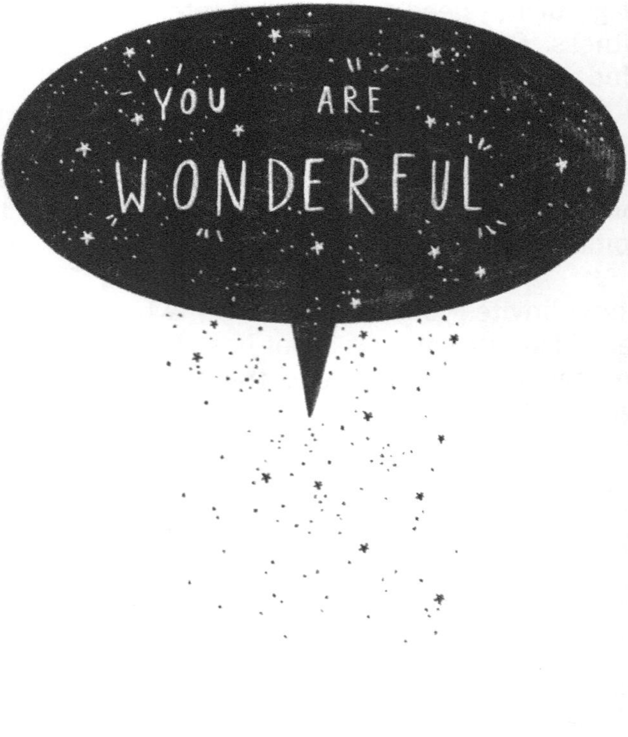
YOU ARE
WONDERFUL

Chapter Six
Reflection

Our Being

"Your understanding is not a powerful contribution to the truth."
A course in miracles.

Reflecting on Being itself.

By now, if you have largely managed to put into practice the Elements In Being, you will be well placed to reflect on the process. What have you learned about yourself and those around you? Are you calmer, more creative, and more inspired? Do you feel more like "yourself"?

Well, if so, then it is more than likely that you have reached a state where you are more connected to the fundamental and final part of yourself, that which is your connection and unhindered access to the space from which all things come. This may be the part where you consider the author has lost the plot! But stay with me for a little while longer.

This space I talk of is much harder to describe because it is not visible, it is not time bound, nor does it appear to be doing anything, yet without it we could not exist. In considering this, please take a moment to keep a mind that is open, to suspend your disbeliefs. I invite you to challenge your own concept of nothingness, emptiness, space or void. I suggest to you that nothingness is actually not only a deceptive description (albeit one that fits with our interpretation of things) but is actually, and conversely everything. Like the space in a vessel without which the vessel could not contain anything. There are many analogies that speak of this, about this requirement of space that allows things to exist, and without which these things could not. The space between the notes without which there would be no music, or the space in the hub of the wheel without which the wheel couldn't turn, or the space inside the house without which there would be no home. In the same way, I suggest that it is not the physical body which is the being but rather it is the space in which the physical body temporarily abides or is manifested. I, and now I hope you, have come to see hints of this unseen "nothingness" which, when our connection to it is opened, allows for peace, love and a complete detachment to ego. This is the pure essential aspect of ourselves as part of a whole in which the universe exists, unpolluted by all the trappings of the material world.

Remember the analogy of a CB radio I used at the beginning of the book. By tuning into our Elements In Being we have tuned into this source as if we were a CB radio. Now consider the control of each one of your Elements as the tuning dial on the radio. As you think, feel and do, you are tuned to the station that feeds back to you your sense of the world. Using the elements available to us, we can rebalance our being by adjusting our thinking, feeling and doing, which has been practiced time and again by people I have encountered and in my own deliberate practice. A good way to think about rebalancing our being is as an opportunity for the essence of ourself to manifest through the space which we allow when we are not unconsciously thinking, feeling and doing.

It is ironic that most of us search for contentment when it is in us all along. We can be content as human beings, though in our modern lives we are ever and increasingly humans thinking and doing. We are humans being done rather than simply being. Time then to allow ourselves to just be. This is so often a bizarre proposition for people to accept. I generally hear an almost flabbergasted "What's the point in that?" Or "How can I possibly just be?" Well, I understand that on the surface it does sound a little, if not significantly dubious, but I hope you have heard me out and have experienced for yourself your own new levels of contentment and Being. I'm not suggesting this is the be all and end all, your ultimate goal, rather a significant principle that you will need to fully understand and continue to practice.

By using the Elements in our Being to understand, observe, allow, accept and then adjust our thoughts, feelings and behaviours, our being can exist peacefully, rather than antagonistically with what is. If we pull back and consider the lack of use of the Elements In Being in our life, then how can we reasonably expect to have well-being? Once you begin to truly understand the power of Being, you will never doubt yourself or indeed the universe again.

Currently, as each year, decade and generation goes by, the ratio of the Being part of us is reducing, and is replaced by more doing and thinking. But these doing and thinking activities are so often the creators and maintainers of anxiety, stress and depression. Now, this pattern of doing and thinking is being supercharged by culture, the internet and social media, your whole Being is liable to sleepwalk, consumed by and into this Matrix. As you have and continue to practice working through this book your being to doing / thinking ratio will gradually increase. Changes will start to occur in various aspects of our lives. You will become more intuitive, more creative, more peaceful, more self reflective, more accepting, more connected with all things, absolutely present. You will be able to put together less obvious connections between ideas and concepts.

Why is this?

I suggest to you that this occurs because, in the state of pure being, we are removing the barriers to these inherent abilities. We have removed the barriers of judgement, rules, our own historical story, emotional triggers and all the years of individual experience which has created a unique lens to look, think and feel through. We are separating and releasing ourselves from our story, and returning to the essence of our humanity. This is a deeply peaceful and contented state to be in.

When it comes down to understanding and examining ourselves, to know what we are, in nearly all cases it seems we are just using our thoughts to do this, but if we are to do this on a deeper level, then thoughts themselves are not enough, we need something else. We need to come to know this in our heart and stomach through an increasing level of being.

I am is the underlying space that we occupy, our Elements In Being are what arise from this space and our thinking is what tries to resolve our uncertainty. However, paradoxically thinking itself generally takes over to assume that "it" is the I am, and in doing so, we become cloaked in a mask which is so great an illusion that we believe it absolutely.

Epilogue

Having now written and experienced the entirety of this book, I would like to note my own particular thoughts about existence, or perhaps what I could otherwise describe as manifestation.

We, like all "things" are made of matter, and all matter exists in a particular form as a parenthesis, an interlude of Being in an eternity of space, consciousness or whatever you choose to call it. Matter is always changing; this is inescapable, and we measure it as time. The hardest materials on earth, even diamonds, are changing on a sub atomic level. Change of form is inescapable and hence continuously new existences or manifestations are created, as old ones are lost. But matter is only one side of ourselves, the side which is time bound, temporary and holds within it, for an interlude, our Being.

"Matter is spirit moving slowly enough to be seen."
Pierre Teilhard de Chardin.

It is the Being part of ourselves, the non-physical which creates our world and that many believe transcends the body. Take this book as an example, where has it come from? It has come from no-thing, the non-physical part of myself has brought together concepts, and arranged them as words on a page through the physical act of typing. These have taken shape, and become reinforced through writing this book, and investigating for myself an explanation of where our Elements In Being "fit" in the universe, both physical and non-physical.

I shall leave the final words of the book to Max Planck who on receiving the Nobel Prize for his work on the atom had this to say;

"All matter originates and exists only by virtue of a force which brings the particles of an atom to vibration and holds this most minute solar system of the atom together. We must assume behind this force the existence of a conscious and intelligent mind. This mind (spirit) is the matrix of all matter."

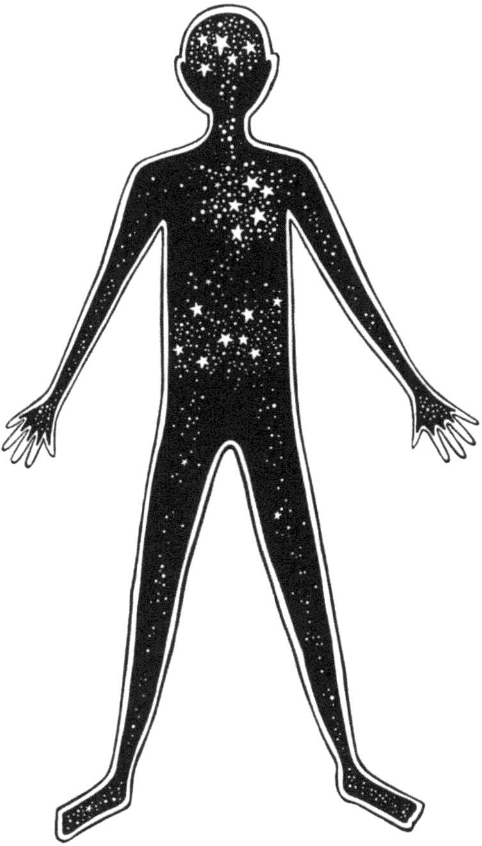

Lightning Source UK Ltd.
Milton Keynes UK
UKHW011424120320
360236UK00001B/11

9 781714 329533